Underwood Lane

John Byrne was born in Paisley in 1940. He worked as a 'slab boy' at AFT Stoddard, the carpet manufacturers, before going to Glasgow School of Art. He became a full-time painter in 1968 following his first London exhibition. His plays include *Nova Scotia*, *Slab Boys*, *Cuttin' a Rug*, *Still Life*, *Writer's Cramp*, *Normal Service*, *Cara Coco* and *Colquhoun and MacBryde*. For TV, he is best known for his BAFTA award-winning series *Tutti Frutti* (adapted for the stage by National Theatre of Scotland, UK tour), and *Your Cheatin' Heart*. He is a distinguished theatre designer and has designed productions for the Traverse Theatre, 7:84, Hampstead Theatre, the Bush Theatre and Scottish Opera.

by the same author

THE SLAB BOYS TRILOGY
The Slab Boys, Cuttin' a Rug, Still Life

COLQUHOUN AND MACBRYDE
TUTTI FRUTTI
NOVA SCOTIA

screenplays
THE SLAB BOYS

JOHN BYRNE

Underwood Lane

faber

First published in 2022
by Faber and Faber Limited
74–77 Great Russell Street
London WC1B 3DA

Typeset by Brighton Gray
Printed and bound in the UK by CPI Group (Ltd), Croydon CR0 4YY

A CIP record for this book
is available from the British Library

978-0-571-37472-4

2 4 6 8 10 9 7 5 3

Underwood Lane was first performed at Johnstone Town Hall, Johnstone, as a co-production between Tron Theatre Company and OneRen with support from Renfrewshire Council's Future Paisley Programme, on 7 July 2022, before transferring to the Tron Theatre, Glasgow, on 14 July 2022. The cast was as follows:

Frankie Sheridan Simon Donaldson
Father Durcan George Drennan
Joey Diamond Scott Fletcher
Maureen Moore Dani Heron
Paula Sheridan Hannah Jarrett-Scott
Dessie Devlin Marc McMillan
Donnatella Fazzi Julia Murray
Eddie Steeples Santino Smith
Bruno Fazzi Harry Ward
Gil Gilfedder Dylan Wood

Director Andy Arnold
Set Designer Becky Minto
Musical Director and Arranger Hilary Brooks
Costume Designer John Byrne and Becky Minto
Lighting Designer Dave Shea
Movement Director Darren Brownlie
Assistant Director Georgia Nelson

Characters

Frankie Sheridan

Father Durcan

Joey Diamond

Maureen Moore

Paula Sheridan

Dessie Devlin

Donnatella Fazzi

Eddie Steeples

Bruno Fazzi

Gil Gilfedder

UNDERWOOD LANE

This text was printed prior to rehearsals for the Tron Theatre production, and some changes may have been made during rehearsals.

Act One

SCENE ONE

Underwood Lane – the winter sun hangs like a suppurating boil glued to a giant sheet of dirty asbestos above the blackened tenements that rear up from the cobbled street like a row of broken teeth and blurts out a 9-carat bellyful of pus onto the undulating rooftops of the lane and those of Darkwood Crescent backing onto it. Underwood Lane is largely Catholic, the crescent staunchly Protestant, which is how come our two protagonists are virtual 'strangers' to one another, Dessie having gone to St Mirin's Academy, Joey to the Abercorn. Donnatella, daughter of Bruno Fazzi, has been privately educated at a convent.

Early morning – the sound of a cello playing an arrangement of 'Her Father Didn't Like Me Anyway' coming from lighted window of Bruno's café.

Enter Dessie in scruffy but 'elegant' Teddy Boy get-up – takes book from drape jacket pocket and drops it into paper bag – Fazzi appears at door of café lugging upright hairdryer and shudders as the icy morning air chills his Mediterranean blood.

Fazzi Cazza Madonna . . .

Dessie Mornin', *Fatso.*

Fazzi Fazzi . . . *Fazzi*! S'Italiano, *si*?? An' it's 'signore' to you . . . capeesh!

Dessie Aye, awright . . . keep yur hair on . . . (*As Fazzi disappears into hairdressing salon.*) *Fatso.*

Dessie gazes up at bedroom window, captivated – eyes closed, listening to the sweet sound of the cello.

(*Opening his eyes – loudly.*) Ho, Donna!

3

Cello stops.

Get yur togs on an' come down the stair . . . thur's
somethin' I want to give you!

> *Donna's face appears at window – she puts a hasty finger
> to her lips and reaches for the blind.*
> *Fazzi rushes out from the salon – bedroom blind drops
> shut.*

Fazzi 'E, you . . . Teddy-bear boy! The only thing ma lassie
want you give hur is a bitta peace 'n' quiet! (*Brandishes
cut-throat razor.*)

> *Enter Father Durcan – he is carrying a load of folding
> chairs.*

Dessie Aw, quit shoutin', I was only . . .

Fazzi (*shouting*) Shutta yur mug or . . . (*Draws razor across
throat – nicking his ear.*) Fa *fangola*, look-a what you
make-a me do!!

Father Durcan (*parking chairs – oblivious*) Ah, Bruno . . .
how are we this fine morning?

Fazzi (*clutching ear*) Aaaaaaargh!!

Dessie Serves you right, *Fatso.*

Father Durcan And how's your mother, Desmond?

Fazzi I facking kill you, Teddy-bear boy!!

Dessie Gonny tell him to chuck swearin' at us, Father?
(*To Fazzi.*) That's the last time I come to your shop furra
fuckin' haircut!

Fazzi What you talking about?? You never been to ma shop
furra fackin' 'aircut! (*To Father Durcan.*) Bon giorno,
Padre, come vai?

Father Durcan (*to Dessie*) Is she up and about again?

Dessie Who . . . ma maw? Naw. (*To Fazzi.*) I huv so been to yur shop!

Father Durcan (*to Dessie*) Has her doctor not suggested anything?

Dessie Aye . . . a trip to Lourdes . . . (*To Fazzi.*) Cost us half-a-dollar, *this*!

Father Durcan *Lourdes?* Christ Almighty . . .

Fazzi What you talk about 'affadolla'?? 'E, Padre, I give you ten quid you say special mass fur departed soul of Donnatella madre . . . she die six year ago this-a mornin' . . . (*Takes out wallet.*) 'Ere, due fiver, va bene?

> *Father Durcan absent-mindedly pockets the two five-pound notes.*
> *Fazzi goes off into salon.*

Father Durcan (*to Dessie*) Will you tell your ma I'll pop in with the Holy Sacrament straight after the Children of Mary coffee mornin' tomorrow lunchtime? (*Loudly.*) Can somebody not gimme a hand with these bloody chairs?? We've got the Knights of St Columba Go-As-You-Please tonight and there's bugger all for the punters to park thur arses on . . . (*Picking chairs up.*) Sufferin' God on the cross . . . (*Exits.*)

> *Donna appears in the street, dressed and with her cello in carrying-bag – she tries sneaking off. Dessie sniffs the air – turns and spots Donna trying to make her getaway.*

Dessie Hang on.

Donna (*nervously looking this way and that*) I'm going to be late for college.

Dessie Here.

> *He tucks paper bag with book inside under her arm.*

It's a book.

Donna I've got a whole library of books upstairs.

Dessie *The Divine Comedy* . . . you'll like it.

Donna I don't particularly like funny books.

Dessie Don't worry, it's not all that funny.

Fazzi reappears from salon.

Fazzi 'E, Donnatella! What I tell you about talkin' wi' *scruff*?

Donna lets paper bag with book inside drop – Dessie picks it up and tucks it back under arm.

Dessie (*fiercely*) You'll like it!

Donna (*setting off*) Ciao, Papa . . . (*Aside to Dessie.*) We have to stop this . . . *please* . . . we have to! (*Over her shoulder to Fazzi.*) I'll be home early for Mamma's anniversary mass. (*Looking from one to the other – loudly.*) Ti amo!

And she's gone – Dessie watches her. Fazzi approaches. A sudden loud BANG! from salon – Fazzi freezes – turns and hurries back to salon. Enter Gil Gilfedder riding butcher boy's bike.

Gil Hi, Des . . . never guess what I picked up on ma travels!

Dessie Aw, naw . . . what wur you told about yur pimply message boy poppin' in furra fried egg roll wi' yur lonely housewife?

Gil parks message bike and takes newspaper-wrapped package from basket.

What the hell's that??

Gil unwraps old dance band guitar, c. 1930s.

Gil What's it look like?

Dessie Give us a clue.

Gil Swappin' it fur an ashet pie an' two black puddin' rings wi' thon big doll that's old man used to play wi the Darkwood Crescent All Stars Jazz Combo . . . *here* . . . (*Handing guitar to Dessie.*) Replace the one yur da flang onty the Farewell Bonfire when he walked out on you an' yur maw.

Dessie hits a chord – a discordant rattle.
Dessie and Joey perform 'Teenager in Love' through next pages.
Enter Father Durcan – picks up more chairs.

Father Durcan Youse'll not be forgetting the old Go-As-You-Please tonight, lads?

Gil You kiddin', Pops? Boy here's armed to the teeth!

Father Durcan Good on you, Gilbert . . . we're lookin' for a coupla musclemen wi' knuckledusters and pickaxe handles to man the doors . . . thur's talk of them bigoted Proddy bastards from up the crescent gatecrashin' the 'Love Thy Neighbour' Excuse Me at the end of the night . . . (*Setting off back to church hall – loudly.*) Three chairs for the bouncers . . . hip, hip . . . (*Exits.*)

Enter Maureen Moore to start work at salon.

Gil Hi, doll . . . fancy a burl round the dance floor?

Maureen (*to Dessie*) Mornin', gorgeous . . . how's tricks?

Dessie ignores her and carries on noodling on guitar.

Gil (*undaunted – a low whistle*) That is one stunnin' outfit yur wearin'.

Dessie Thanks.

Gil No' yours . . . *hurs*.

Maureen (*surly*) S'what I wear every mornin' . . . you blind or somethin'? (*To Dessie.*) Paula Sheridan's boyfriend's got himself a brand-new Hofner President. She reckons he's goin' to wipe the floor with it at this Go-As-You-Please carry-on tonight.

Dessie What is it, some kinda new-fangled mop?

Maureen Pardon me? (*To Gil.*) What you snortin' at?

Dessie Hofner whatsitsname . . . some kinda . . . ?

Maureen Naw, it's one of them big guitars with the f-holes and . . . (*Penny drops.*) Och, see you. (*To Gil.*) 'Some kinda new-fangled mops' . . . don't you think that's hilarious? (*To Dessie.*) That is hilarious! Hey, listen . . . ma date's fell through for tonight so if you find yourself at a loose end . . . ?

Dessie 'Loose end'? (*Checks his rear.*)

Maureen (*moving off – to herself*) . . . 'Some kinda new-fangled mop' . . . wait till I tell Paula, she'll end hursell! (*Over shoulder.*) Catch you later, Des.

Gil (*calling after her*) If you need a lift after yur work, doll, I've got maself some transport.

Fazzi appears from salon – spots Maureen.

Fazzi 'E, Marina, donna pit yur customer napper unner that 'airdryer . . . she blaw the heid affy them!

Maureen Aw, naw, I've got a perm at nine an' a double-bookin' fur a Marcel wave at ten, what'll I tell them??

Fazzi Don' tell them nuffink, I fix-a the bugger!

Enter Joey Diamond with Paula Sheridan in tow – Joey does some ostentatious rubber-necking like he's never been in this neighbourhood (which he hasn't). Paula's brother Frankie brings up the rear, a big swanky guitar case in his mitt. Paula is carrying a funeral wreath. Joey casts a jaundiced eye in the direction of the café.

Joey 'Bruno's'? Doll like you shouldny huv to work in a dump like that.

Paula Furst chance I get I'm jackin' it in . . . (*Sniffing the air.*) D'you smell somethin' burnin'?

Joey Yeh . . . it's ma red hot smoulderin' love fur you, babe . . . c'mere.

Paula (*to Gil*) What *you* starin' at?

Joey C'mere, I said!

Pulls Paula close and nuzzles her throat.

Paula (*giggling*) Chuck it, thur's folk watchin'!

Joey Let them watch . . . see if I care. (*Starts with the nuzzling again.*)

Frankie goes walkabout – has a nose around Gil's message bike – Gil keeps a watchful eye on Joey. Likewise Dessie, but less obviously. Maureen has a mooch around, then wanders over.

Joey (*breaks off mid-nuzzle*) What was that??

Paula Aw, naw . . . I was really enjoyin' maself . . . what was what?

Dessie carries on playing.

Joey *That.*

He casts around – spots Dessie and breaks away from Paula.

(*To Frankie.*) Ho!

Frankie pockets butchermeat from Gil's bike – saunters over. Maureen joins Paula.

Maureen Hey, Paula . . . you hear the one about yur boyfriend an' his 'new-fangled *whatsitsname*'?

Paula His new-fangled *what*?

Frankie opens guitar case and hands Joey his Hofner President. Gil's eyes almost pop out of his head. He gives Dessie a nudge. Frankie places small amplifier on ground.

Maureen (*trying not to laugh*) Ask Des, it was him that told us it.

Paula Des who?

Joey plugs his Hofner into amp and adds a couple of licks.

Maureen Him there . . . an' chuck starin', he's *booked*.

Paula Good God, I've seen healthier-lookin' specimens crawlin' out from under a rock.

Joey and Dessie end their impromptu 'set' with Joey adding a show-offy flourish.

Frankie (*applauding*) Aw, how cool was that?? Cheers, Joey.

Joey (*aside*) Can it, ya clown!

Fazzi emerges from salon, wiping back of his hand over his forehead.

Fazzi 'E, Marina?? That's yur dryer workin' . . . away in an' donna futter wi' nuthin', eh?

Paula Mornin', Mr Fazzi.

Fazzi 'E Paola! Where you be??

Paula Sorry I'm late but me an' Joey stopped off at thon wee fruit shop in Well Street to get yur wife somethin' . . . (*Produces wreath from behind her back.*) Sorry, yur *late* wife.

Fazzi takes wreath – Paula giggles.

. . . Funny, isn't it?

Fazzi (*gazing at wreath – clearly moved*) Naw, naw . . . s'a very nice.

Paula Naw, I mean hur an' I . . . the pair of us . . . me an' Mrs Fazzi . . . *both* bein' late, yeh?

> *Fazzi crosses himself – turns his face heavenwards and murmurs a prayer.*
> *Maureen plants herself in salon doorway, arms folded – and* glowers.

(*To Joey.*) Didny get it, did he? You thought it was funny, didn't you, lover boy?

Joey I think everythin' you do is comical, sweetheart.

> *Joey passes Hofner to Frankie – Paula starts towards café.*

Paula (*to Joey*) Mind an' bring ma good frock when you come to pick us up . . . oh, an' ma shoes, *not* the slingbacks, ma other pair, thur under the bed-settee in the back bedroom, tell ma mammy . . .

> *Gil, smitten, is watching her every move.*

Paula (*to Gil*) . . . What you starin' at?? (*To Frankie.*) Goin' to tell him to chuck starin' at us? (*Sets off for café.*)

Frankie (*to Gil*) That's ma young sister, you.

Gil Yur jokin'. (*Turning to stare.*)

Frankie Chuck starin' at hur, well!

Paula You can forget about havin' to fix that plug on the jukebox, Mr Fazzi, I've stuck a big screwdriver in the socket an' wired it up to the cooker . . . works a treat. (*To Maureen at door of hairdressing salon.*) Is it awright if I pop in after dinner time an' get you to backcomb this fur us?

Maureen (*frostily*) Wur fully booked . . . thur's a big do on at Our Lady of the Seven Dolours this evening and wur dryer's on the blink . . . sorry.

Paula (*looking Maureen up and down*) You want to ask the boss to get you a new overall, you look like a bagga tautties in that effort. (*Loudly, to Joey.*) The black patents wi' the heel grips, tell ma mother! (*Disappears inside café.*)

At far end of the street Joey and Frankie are in a huddle while Dessie and Gil feign a certain indifference in the wake of the 'duel'.

Fazzi (*coming out of his reverie*) 'E, Paola . . . where you are? Paola!

Paula appears at café door, overall in hand – disgruntled.

Paula Quit shoutin'! What is it??

Fazzi (*holding wreath aloft and wiping a tear away*) Ma beloved Maria . . . she no' furget this.

Paula (*donning overall – softening*) Och, away . . . she was a lovely person. I mind hur givin' our Frankie a pokey hat an' a whole box of Black Magic choclits out the van when his flute fell down the stank at the Orange Walk one year . . . (*Loudly.*) Is that no' right Frankie! She was dead lovely, wasn't she??

Fazzi (*squinting along the street*) Whit wan's wee Frankie?

Paula Besides, the guy in the fruit shop had put it out fur the bin motor . . . the wreath . . . never cost us a tosser. (*Leaning out of café doorway – to Maureen.*) You absolutely positive you couldn't fit us in furra . . .?

Maureen I told you, wur fully booked.

She looks Paula up and down – they are wearing matching overalls. Maureen shoos customer into salon.

Paula *and* **Maureen** (*as they exeunt*) Bitch!

Fazzi wanders off in direction of Boys' Club.

Fazzi 'E, Padre . . . where you go? Padre . . .?

Joey and Dessie slowly circle the combat area while Frankie and Gil look on.

Joey So . . . I know yur face, right?

Dessie Could do. Hud it fur ages.

Joey Wur we at the school together, mebbe?

Dessie Not unless you wur studyin' fur the priesthood, naw.

Joey (*turning to Frankie*) 'Not unless you wur studyin' fur the priesthood' . . . dig him.

Frankie lets out a guffaw – Joey gives him a look. Frankie clams up.

(*To Gil.*) Your features ring a bell an' all . . . right, Frankie?

Frankie (*unsure*) Er . . .

Joey Frankie's been away furra while.

Gil On yur holidays, yeh?

Frankie In the Borstal.

Gil Oh.

Joey So . . . er. Sorry, what'd you say yur name was again?

Dessie I never.

Gil It's Dessie . . . Dessie Devlin.

Dessie draws Gil a sinker.

Joey Thanks, pal . . . (*To Dessie.*) You the Devlin that's maw's got cancer of the jaw?

Dessie Who told you that?

Joey Cannae remember . . . must be somebody else's maw. So . . . Dessie . . .

Gil (*peeved*) You never told us yur maw had cancer of the jaw, ya rotten bastart.

Dessie You heard the guy . . . must be somebody else's maw.

Gil (*unconvinced*) Aye, right.

Dessie (*to Joey*) sorry about that. Where wur we?

Joey So . . . *Dessie* . . .

Dessie So what? *Joey?*

Joey stretches out a hand to Frankie, palm upturned. Frankie places a coin on it.

Joey . . . it's your call.

Dessie Tails.

Joey flips the coin, catches it, slaps it down on the back of his other hand – Dessie, Frankie and Gil crane forward.

Gil Good shout, Des. (*Sotto voce.*) Wish I knew what the hell was happenin' here.

Joey (*uncovers coin – smiles*) I get to choose the name, right?

Gil Naw, sorry, I'm completely lost . . . what 'name'? Don't tell us you an' him's went an' got big Donna up the duff?

Dessie Remind me to batter your melt in, Gilfedder . . . (*To Joey.*) Once we've shook on it, that's it, right?

Joey Bindin' contract, yeh.

Sticks out his hand – Dessie hesitates for a moment, then takes Joey's hand – they shake.

Gil (*genially – to Frankie*) That's you an' me left in the dark, d'you want to go fur a bagga chips?

Frankie (*grabbing Gil's lapels*) Furget the chips, you an' yur pal's jist chose to embark upon a musical odyssey wi' me an' Joey Diamond. I'm yur Road Manager, so . . .?

Gil Wur in furra a bumpy ride, yeh?

Frankie Got it in one, kiddo.

*A loud BANG from the café – all heads turn as Paula,
her hair all over the shop, face black, stumbles into view.*

Paula *Mr Fazzi?!*

Blackout.
  Slow lights up.
  *Song: 'Crying in the Rain' – Dessie and Joey on
guitars, Gil on harmonica . . .*
  Lights down.

SCENE TWO

*Later that same morning – Dessie's bedroom – cramped and
untidy. Joey reclines on unmade single bed – Paula attempts
to rectify the damage to her coiffure in scabby mirror while
Frankie prowls around, picking stuff up and peering at it.*

Joey Listen, if yur half as good as yur bree there says then
yur in, right?

Paula What you listenin' to him fur? I only took it up cos
ma da bought us a big roary sash wi' King Billy's horse on
it an' a paira red white an' blue shorts wi' cute wee bows at
the side . . . what you gettin' us inty, Frankie Sheridan??

Frankie Ho, dig this, Joey.

*Holds up statue of Virgin Mary – presses button on base
– the stars of the Virgin's Crown and robes wink on and
off. A tinny voice sings: 'Dark night has come down to
this rough spoken world and the Banners of Darkness
are boldly unfurl'd . . .'*
  *Enter Dessie – grabs statue from Frankie and gives
him a shove.*

Ho! Watch who yur shovin'!

Joey (*getting up from bed*) Cool it, Frankie boy.

Dessie replaces statue.

How's yur maw?

Dessie Fine. What's she doin' here? (*Nodding at Paula.*)

Joey She's wur drummer.

Dessie She's wur what??

Paula 'Scuse me, but 'she' happens to huv a name. (*To Dessie.*) The name's Paula . . . furget it an' yur dead. (*Exits.*)

Paula (*off*) Sticks! (*Pops her head round door.*) Thur should be a pair of drumsticks in the drawer where ma da keeps his marshal's truncheon . . . Bye. (*Disappears.*)

Joey What time'll we make it??

Dessie Make what?

Joey Wur run-through.

Dessie Aw . . . er . . .

Joey Go-As-You-Please-Yurself's at nine . . . say four o'clock? (*To Frankie.*) That give you enough time to get the gear?

Frankie Bags.

Joey You want Frankie should pick up whatsisname's bass fiddle?

Dessie Naw, naw, he lives jist next door to the Boys' Club.

Joey (*opening door*) Four, yeh?

Dessie Numbers? No' sure I've got all the words wrote out fur . . .

Exit Frankie.

Joey Four *o'clock*, Dessie . . . the café, yeh?

Dessie Aw. Yeh, sure, Joey.

*Exit Joey. Dessie takes the photograph of Donna from
his pocket – lowers himself onto the bed.*
  Song: 'Garden of Eden' – Dessie and band, off.
  Lights down.

SCENE THREE

*Lights up on Dessie's bedroom – early afternoon. Dessie at
the window looking down into the street – Gil sitting
disconsolately on the bed, staring at picture of Sacred Heart
opposite.*

Dessie Don't see yur butcherboy's message bike down here,
Gil. Where'd you park it?

Gil Didny park it nowhere . . . an' fur why? Cos I don't
huv a butcherboy's message bike.

Dessie You had one this mornin'. Don't tell us you went
under a bus wi' it?

Gil Worse. Chrichton the Butcher took it back off us.

Dessie Lost his licence again, has he?

Gil Eh?

Dessie Drink drivin', yeh?

Gil Naw . . . two old bags phones the shop to complain
about not getting' thur butcher-meat orders.

Dessie The bastards.

Gil Commandeered the machine soon as I got back off ma
round . . . wumman on the bacon slicer said I could huv
him hauled up before a tribunal.

Dessie (*looking to and fro along the street*) Huv who
hauled up?

Gil Chrichton the bloody Butcher! Who is it yur lookin' fur down there anyhow?

Dessie (*spotting his quarry*) Aha! (*Calling down to street below.*) Hullo! Ho! Up Here! . . . Naw . . . *here*! It's me . . . Dessie! Come on up, I need to see you desperately . . . Naw, it canny wait, I'm comin' down to get you! (*Shuts window and crosses to door.*) C'mon, Gilfedder, when I've got a song in the Top Twenty I'll buy you a bloody message bike. (*Pausing at door.*) You wur too old to be a butcherboy anyhow. (*Exits.*)

> *Gil sits there staring at Sacred Heart picture – gives an involuntary shudder.*

Gil (*to Sacred Heart*) Chuck starin' at us, well!

> *A bell tinkles somewhere in the house – Gil gets up, crosses to door – closes it. Returns to bed – sits. Another tinkle. Gil sits staring at Sacred Heart. Another tinkle, more urgent this time.*

Aw, shut yur face!

> *Silence. A few moments later Dessie enters – stands by the door. Donna enters shyly carrying her cello in its canvas bag. Dessie takes it from her and motions Gil to stand up – Gil stands up and moves away from the bed, his eyes glued to Donna. Dessie lays the cello carefully on the bed. Gil squats down on a pile of books.*

Dessie Give us yur coat off.

Donna No, no, I can't stay, my dad'll be . . .

Dessie C'mon, yur dad'll no' be phonin' the polis jist yet . . . (*Helps her off with coat – chucks it on the bed.*) You know Gill.

Donna I told him I'd be home early . . . Hi, Gilbert . . . what is it that's so important it couldn't wait till . . . ?

Dessie Hang on . . . where're yur manners, you? (*Hauls Gil to his feet.*) Per favore, signorina.

Donna gives a little laugh at the charming use of her mother tongue and lowers herself onto the 'chair' – her knees come up rather indecorously to meet her chin.

I'll move you across to the bed in a minute . . . wuv got about an hour.

Donna An *hour*? What for?

Gil (*getting wrong end of stick*) D'you want me go, yeh?

Dessie Naw!

Donna I can't possibly stay here for . . . (*Struggling to get up.*) Oooow!

Dessie (*crossing to bed*) Okay, let's call it twenty minutes.

Gil Naw, I'm definitely fur the off.

Dessie Hang around, Gilfedder, I promise yur goin' to learn quite a lot.

Gil turns to face the wall.

Donna (*on all fours*) I shouldn't be here . . .

Dessie C'mon, sweetheart, you can spare ten minutes, surely . . . (*Starts unzipping cello bag.*)

Donna freezes – Gil shudders.

. . . jist as long as you manage to teach the boy there how to master the bass fiddle, wuv got a rehearsal at . . . (*Zip jams.*) Bugger!

Gil *and* **Donna** What??

Gil I've never even *saw* a bass fiddle, never heed *mastered* one!

Dessie Awright, awright, furget 'master', let's settle fur 'rudimentary grasp of' . . .

Donna gets to her feet, marches to bed – shoves Dessie aside, grabs her cello and stomps towards the door.

. . . Hold on . . .

Exit Donna.

. . . Donna?

Front door slams shut.

Gil That happened to be a cello, by the way.

Dessie (*angrily*) I know it was a . . . (*Stops – lowering his voice – fiercely.*) I know it was a bloody cello! It works along the same lines as . . . (*Stops abruptly and listens.*) She didn't happen to ring hur bell while I was down the stair, did she?

Gil Yur maw? Uh-uh . . . not that I heard.

Dessie (*talking normally*) Good. She must be havin' a snooze. (*Picks Donna's coat up.*)

Song: 'You're So Square', unplugged – Dessie and wee band, off.

SCENE FOUR

The back room of Fazzi's café – Joey leans against the burnt-out jukebox noodling away with his Hofner. Paula tos and fros in the café proper with frothy coffees, ice-cream floats, etc., for the motley crew of dolls and corner boys who come and go. Frankie waits outside in the street for Dessie and Gil who are late. Paula's drum kit – snare on a stand and a hi-hat – is set up in the back room waiting for her to practise on.

Eddie Steeples – dressed in too-big black camelhair coat and dark glasses – wanders through from café with his coffee. He does a bit of cool finger-popping to Joey's guitar before Joey notices him and stops playing.

Steeples That was cookin', man . . . Eddie Steeples . . . used to run about wi' yur brother George . . . lemme give you ma card. (*Puts coffee down – hunts through pockets.*) Nice guy, George . . . went to watch the Pirates play hockey, done a bitta skatin' together . . . (*Still hunting through his pockets for cards.*) What's he up to these days? Huvny bumped into him in God knows how long . . . is he still in the motor trade?

Joey He's in the jail.

Steeples (*discovering a business card in his wallet*) Aha . . . there you go. (*Hands it to Joey.*) I've wrote ma office number on the back, movin' into new premises on Monday . . . the jail, did you say? Canny say I'm surprised . . . he was always a bitty a bad egg.

Joey (*reading from card*) 'Credit With Dignity' . . . what's that mean?

Steeples Means I've gave you the wrong card, dinnit? (*Takes it back – finds another card.*) Here . . . try that fur size.

Joey takes the card.

Wuv got connections Down South an' most of mainland Europe . . . last thing we done was a big package tour wi' Buddy Knox an' Howlin' Wolf . . .

Joey You mean the real Buddy Knox? The one that done 'Party Doll'?

Steeples Course . . . what d'you take me fur?

Enter Paula from café.

Couldny vouch fur Howlin' bein' a real wolf either but that's showbiz, innit?

Joey Any sign, doll?

Paula Naw . . . (*To Steeples.*) S'this your cup? (*Retrieves coffee cup.*) I could tell they wurny gonny come. (*To Steeples.*) Is it the toilets yur lookin' fur?

Steeples (*raised dark glasses – peering at Paula*) An' who ur you supposed to be?

Joey She's supposed to be wur drummer but wur two dummies short of a combo at the moment so . . .

Enter Frankie.

Frankie The pair of them's jist came round the corner, d'you want us to give them a doin'?

Steeples Is that you, Frankie?

Frankie Or we could jist make it a verbal, seein' as how it's . . . Christ, Eddie Steeples . . . huvny saw you since where'd-you-cry-it . . .

Steeples 'Bag O'Nails', West Hartlepool . . . how you doin', son?

Frankie I've done better . . . what you doin' back here?

Steeples Bitta this, bitta that . . .

Paula (*to Joey*) D'you know this guy?

Joey (*shrugs*) Who ever really knows anybody, doll?

Paula Aw, that's very helpful, that is.

Steeples (*to Frankie*) What you up to?

Enter Dessie and Gil – Dessie carries a scruffy guitar bag while Gil is lugging a large wooden box and a length of pole.

Gil Hiya . . . sorry wur late but . . . God, this's heavy . . .

He lowers it to the floor and bends forward, leaning his elbows on the box – knackered. Paula exits to café.

Joey I hope this isny what I think it is.

Dessie C'mon, his real one's in the pawn.

Frankie What you got in the box, Jim?

Joey (*to Gil*) Ho, this isny the Boy Scouts' jamboree yuv joined!

 Steeples wanders over to Dessie.

Steeples Eddie Steeples . . . You must be . . .?

Dessie (*taking guitar out of the bag*) Buggered? Naw, I got the bus back . . . Gilfedder there hud to lug that aw the way from Foxbar . . . what'd you say yur name was . . . Steeples?

Steeples I'd give you ma card but I've jist ran out . . . (*Admiring guitar.*) Nice daud of maple yuv got there. I know where I can get a tremolo arm fur that.

Dessie Not all that sure I want to swap it furra tremolo arm.

Steeples Buckshee.

Dessie Naw, I know that particular make . . . I definitely don't want to swap.

 Slings guitar round his neck.

Ho, Frankie boy? Where's this amp you promised us?

 Gil is putting together his tea chest bass.

Gil Am I getting' an amp?

Joey (*loudly*) Paula! Get you in here!

 Frankie crosses to Dessie with an amplifier the size of a
 small biscuit tin – plugs lead from amp into Dessie's
 guitar pick-up.

Frankie When that rid light comes on that's you ready to rock'n'roll . . . naw, hold on till she warms up . . .

Enter Paula, sloughing off her overall and addressing
what's left of the corner boys and dolls in the café proper.

Paula . . . Naw, wur no' servin' any more iced drinks or
coffees, wur shut, right?? (*Turns – spots Gil with tea chest
bass.*) Aw, heh . . . that's really cute! You seen this, Joey . . .
it's really cute, innit?

Joey (*seething*) You say any more an' wur getting' you a
kazoo an' a washboard!

Paula Great! God, this is goin' to be a right laugh!

She gets behind her makeshift kit – she and Gil take off
into an improvised 'jam'.
Song: 'You're So Square' – Dessie and full band,
production number.
Steeples and Frankie the roadie contribute an
impromptu jive – dolls and corner boys drift through
from the café and before you know it the joint is jumpin'.
In the melee of gyrating corner boys and boppin' dolls
suddenly there's Donna, lured down from upstairs by the
infectious noise, shedding her 'Virgin Mary' image and
surrendering herself to the wild and wanton joy of the
jive – Steeples and Frankie partnering her in turn.
Soon Donna and co are the main attraction – the
corner boys and dolls gathering round to egg them on.
Just as the music and the jive reach a crescendo the
sound cuts out dead – there stands Bruno Fazzi, face like
thunder – a plug dangling from his mitt. A chorus of jeers
and catcalls.

Fazzi Basta! Basta!

Silence falls.

Whadda fack you think you play at?? Is anniversary my
wife die . . . I godda Padre say special mass upstair in ma
livin' room, 'e canny 'ear 'is facking ear! (*Confronting
Donna – in Italian.*) What in God's name do you think you

are doing?? Your mother is lookin' down from Heaven right now, tears of shame burning her eyes . . . the beautiful child she brought into the world has turned into a whore in front of the whole street! (*Grabbing hold of his daughter's wrist.*) I spit on you like you spit upon the memory of my beloved wife!

He spits into Donna's cupped hand – turns on his heel and barges his way through the crowd of dolls and corner boys.

Dessie Ya bastart!

He rushes forward to get at Fazzi – Donna steps between Dessie and her father.

Donna (*restraining Dessie*) No, Dessie, don't . . . please . . . he's right, I should've stayed upstairs . . .

Dessie What for?? Yur maw's dead, Donna. What you gonny do . . . spend the rest of yur days on yur knees when you could be jivin'?

He pulls her suddenly to him and kisses her clumsily but with passion – lets her go. They stare into one another's faces like they've just been in a car crash.

Life or death, Donna . . . what's it goin' to be?

Donna closes her eyes – Dessie waits . . . and waits.
Donna opens her eyes wide and launches herself at Dessie.

Dessie *and* **Donna** Aaaaaaaaaaaaaargh!

They share a long lingering embrace.
Enter Gil – squeezes past, his tea chest bass dismantled.

Gil Whoops . . . mind ma brush handle . . . (*To Donna.*) Nifty bitta jitterbuggin', doll. Shame yur old man didnae altogether dig it, but there you go. (*Sets off – stops.*) Haw,

Dessie . . . boy Steeples wants you to go stick yur autograph on a bitta paper . . . Joey Diamond's gave him his . . . I've gave him mines . . . Frankie canny write right, so I put a cross fur his moniker, an' I'm no' too sure about wur drummer . . . (*Loudly.*) Ho, you there, Paula? (*Exits.*)

> *Dessie and Donna break gently apart.*
> *Song: 'That's Amore', acoustic – Dessie and Donna duet.*

SCENE FIVE

Dessie's bedroom – late at night two days later. Dessie lies in bed looking up at the ceiling. Bedroom door opens and Donna comes in – she is carrying her cello and a bulging holdall. Dessie sits in bed.

Dessie I thought you wur never comin' back you wur away that long . . . What kept you?

Donna (*dumping luggage*) I had to hide across the street till I saw him going out. Took me ages to find the key . . . I'm frozen!

Dessie (*throwing cover back*) Get yur togs off an' come in, I'll warm you up . . .

Donna Did you go see Father Durcan?

Dessie . . . Er . . . didn't have to . . . he came here wi' a two-gallon flagon of Holy Water, chucked it everywhere . . . him an' I said the 'De Profundis' an' I hud a word wi' him about . . . you know . . . you an' I . . . he's goin' to read out the banns at twelve o'clock mass this Sunday comin'.

Donna Good.

> *She kicks off her shoes, slips off her coat – undresses quickly – puts coat back on and climbs into bed beside Dessie.*

It's freezing!

She pulls coat collar up round her ears – shivering.

Dessie (*folds coat collar back to see Donna's face*) Trust this isny a trailer fur wur honeymoon? (*Kisses her.*)

Donna What time's the funeral at?

Dessie Ten o'clock. (*Makes to kiss her again.*)

Donna Waaaaaaaaaaaaaaaaa!

She throws covers back and leaps out of bed.

Dessie Ten o'clock in the *mornin'* . . . hur coffin's still next door, fur God's sake.

Donna It wasn't that . . .

She drops to her knees.

. . . I forgot to say my prayers. (*Crossing herself.*) 'Hail Mary, full of grace, the Lord is with thee . . .'

Dessie (*sinks back onto pillow*) Now it's the trailer fur *The Nun's Story* . . . might as well join hur . . . (*Shuts his eyes.*) It's is seven years since my last confession and these are my sins . . . I was foolish enough to believe that when I furst clapped eyes on St Theresa there that one day I would be lyin' in bed in ma shurt tail . . . ma maw would be lyin' through the wall in hur box so I'd be safe in the knowledge that ma bedroom door wasny gonny fly open any minute so that hur an' I . . . (*As Donna lands on top of him.*) Aaaayah, bugger!

Donna I've finished my prayers now.

Dessie (*winded*) Right, get the coat off . . .

Lights down.
Laughter in the dark.
Song: 'Three Steps to Heaven' segues into 'Love Me Tender', a capella – ensemble.

Underwood Lane – next morning. Dessie's mother's coffin is conveyed along Underwood Lane to the church of Our Lady of the Seven Dolours – Father Durcan heads the cortège, intoning prayers for the dead according to the Latin rite.

Bruno Fazzi, standing outside his hairdressing salon with his trainee assistant Maureen by his side, removes his headgear and bows his head – Maureen wipes away a tear.

Enter Joey and Paula from far end of street.

Paula Aw . . . look . . . a real live funeral!

Joey So that's how come he never showed up, I get it now.

Paula I wonder whose it is? (*Loudly, to Maureen.*) Cooeee! Who was it kicked the bucket?

Joey Can it, or I'll bop you one! Where's yur sensitivity??

Paula Went the same road as ma virginity . . . on the same night, or don't you recall?

Dessie appears at the entrance to number 7 – pale and withdrawn, his one concession is a black scarf knotted around his throat while Donna, on the other hand is dressed entirely in black from head to feet.

Dessie gives Joey a curt nod – Paula peels off.

Joey (*falling into step with Dessie behind the coffin*) I was comin' to chin you about yur 'no-show' at the Go-As-You-Please last night but we'll leave that fur another time.

Dessie Gee, thanks.

Joey Yur maw, yeh?

Dessie I only discovered she'd gave up the ghost when I went back up the stair after the run-through . . . hud to wait fur the quack to come an' sign hur death certificate. (*Stops to light cigarette.*) Got the daft bugger to phone the Co-operative undertakers when he got back to his surgery.

Cortège moves on – Dessie and Joey linger. Paula darts across.

Paula They say it was some old bag that hud cancer . . . somebody give us a light, I'm chitterin'. (*To Joey.*) What you lookin' at us like that fur? I've only got ma vest on under this!

Dessie I would've sent word but you know how it is.

Joey Furget it.

Dessie How did you do as a trio? Huvny seen Gilfedder to ask him.

Joey We came fourth behind a banjo picker, a 'boy soprano' . . . an' a guy wi' a club foot that wore his suit back-to-front an' sang 'Jezebel'.

Dessie That isny too bad, considerin' . . .

Joey Considerin' they thought we wur a skiffle group, you mean? (*Glancing at Paula.*) Yeh . . . not too bad.

Fazzi crosses behind the smokers – spots Dessie and Donna – spits on the ground. Donna draws closer to Dessie. Maureen crosses from salon.

Maureen I'm awful sorry to hear about yur mother, Des. I would've worn black but since I never ever met hur I didny think it would entirely appropriate . . . (*To Donna.*) Aw, never noticed you there. You must be the boss's daughter? We've never actually met . . . Maureen Moore . . . known to Des as 'Mo' . . . nice to meet you at long last. Dessie an' me huv been close friends fur donkey's. (*Fingering funeral frock.*) Forgive me askin' but did you run this up yurself? Oh-oh . . . (*Reaches down and pulls at thread on hem.*) there you go. Don't want yur hem comin' down an' sendin' you flyin' inty his mother's casket.

As Maureen moves off, Gil comes galloping down the street – dishevelled.

Gil Christ, sorry, Dessie . . . I only jist seen it in last night's paper . . . ten o'clock, it said. What time is it now?? (*To Maureen.*) Aw, hi, Mo, that's . . . er . . . that's yur overall from the hairdresser's, innit? (*To Paula.*) Mornin', beautiful . . . classy bitta schmutter you've got on . . . (*To Dessie.*) I would've chapped yur door after the Talent Show . . . which was a disaster, by the way . . . but I thought you an' hur might be . . . you know . . . *busy*, yeh? (*To Donna.*) As fur you, gorgeous . . . words fail me . . . *wow*!

Father Durcan appears from church.

Father Durcan We're just about to start, Desmond.

Dessie Just comin', Father . . . (*To Gil.*) Make sure you're sittin' behind a *pillar*, okay?

Takes Donna's arm – they cross to join Father Durcan.

Gil (*to Maureen*) No' wish you hud a figure like that? Check out the *gams*! (*Loudly.*) Ho, wait fur me! (*Hurries after Dessie and Donna.*)

Joey (*to Paula*) You don't want to go in, do you, doll?

Paula Who . . . me? Into a *chapel*??

Joey Please yurself.

Sets off after Dessie and Donna – Paula stands there looking poleaxed.

Maureen (*as Joey disappears into church*) I could take you fur that shampoo 'n' set, if you fancy?

Song: 'Three Steps to Heaven', reprise.

Underwood Lane – six months later. A notice in the window of the café reads: 'For Sale' – the one in the window of the hairdresser reads: 'Closing Down – Shampoo and Set ½ Price'.

Enter Donna looking pale and drawn – she is struggling with heavy groceries. She walks slowly along the street – stops outside number 7.

Donna (*calling up to window*) Dessie? (*Loudly.*) Are you there, Dessie?!

Enter a double-bass at opposite end of street – it advances along the street – stops.

It's me!

Gil appears from behind double-bass.

Gil He should be in, doll . . . (*Parks double-bass – joins Donna.*) you there, Dessie?? Ho . . . it's yur *missus*!

Donna (*calling up to window*) It's your *fiancée*! Are you going to come down??

Gil Here, let me give you a hand up with stair wi' them bags, gorgeous.

Donna No, I want him to do it, it was him that got me pregnant, not you.

Gil Wish it had been me.

Donna What?

Gil Nuthin'.

Gil *and* **Donna** (*together*) Deeeeeeeeeeeesie!

Enter Dessie carrying guitar bag – joins Gil and Donna.

Gil, Donna *and* **Dessie** (*up at window*) Deeeeeeeeeeeeeeesie!

Dessie Naw, bugger's definitely not in.

Donna (*rounding on him*) Where the hell've you been??

Gil Aye, where the hell've you been? You left before me an' I hud to walk back here luggin' that monstrosity.

Dessie produces a bottle of Chianti and a small parcel.

Dessie 'Happy Birthday to you . . . happy birthday to you . . .'

Donna (*melting – to Gil*) He remembered! (*Throwing arms around Dessie.*) You remembered!

Enter Steeples. Dessie and Donna go into a clinch.

Steeples Stuck ma noodle round yur rehearsal room door, musta jist missed you guys. (*To Gil.*) How you getting' on wi' yur big doodah?

Gil Aye, awright . . . jist canny get ma big doodah on the bus, Eddie.

Steeples Ask Frankie to saw a daud off yur big doodah an' if that disny work wull get you a set o' maracas an' your own transport, how's that? 'Scuse me . . . not wishin' for to interrupt the loveburds but . . .

Gil It's hur burthday.

Steeples Whose burthday?

Gil Hurs . . . Donna.

Steeples Donna? Aw . . . that Donna.

Dessie and Donna break apart reluctantly.

Dessie What can we do fur you, Eddie?

Steeples (*checks his watch*) Many happy returns, hen . . . Not wantin' to rush you or nuthin', Des, it's jist that I've got the A and R guy from one of the biggest record labels in

the country sittin' waitin' fur us in The Rosebud bar . . .
very anxious to meet you . . .

Dessie Yur kiddin'.

Steeples . . . Cross ma heart an' hope to die in the Bar-L.
He's flew in special . . . picked him up personally at
Prestwick aerodrome maself . . . got to get him back there
before . . . (*Checks watch.*) *Jesus*, . . . anyhow, he's broke
his trip to the States an' done himself an' us a favour in
response to them tapes I sent him that you an' the boys
done of yur songs . . . pardon me . . . that you an' the boys
an' whatshername done of yur songs, yeh?

Dessie God, that's fantastic . . . the only thing is . . .

Steeples Naw, naw, I realise you want to spend the evenin'
wi' yur lady love here but it's now or never, Dessie son . . .
thur's a coupla hot young songwriters in New York that
would not only give thur own eyeteeth but the eyeteeth of
thur wifes an' weans jist to get a sniffa this boy's oxter
cologne . . .

Donna You've got to go and meet him, Des . . .

Dessie I know, but what about . . .

Donna My birthday can wait, this chap's plane obviously
can't. It's your dream come true. And mine. Do it for me . . .
yeh?

> *Dessie dithers – Steeples agitatedly checks his watch
> again.*

For your mother then . . . it was her dream too. Unless you
were telling me lies? Dessie?

Steeples C'mon, you heard the doll . . . if you don't want to
do it fur hur, do it fur yur maw. (*Taking Dessie's arm.*) Let's
go, I've got a taxi rackin' up a fortune at the end of the
street yonner. (*Over shoulder.*) You look after the burd, Gil,
see that she behaves hursell.

He hurries Dessie off. Donna rips parcel open – a silk scarf.

Gil D'you think you will but?

Donna Will but what? (*Waving Dessie off.*) Thanks for the lovely present!

Gil Behave yurself? (*Loudly.*) Don't sign nuthin' t'you see the big bagga dosh, Dessie!

Tootle of taxi horn – Donna slips birthday present round her throat.

Donna I'm expecting a baby in three months, what d'you think I'm going to do . . . climb onto the roof and dive naked into an eggcupfull of Chianti?

Gil If you've got the eggcup, doll, I've got . . . (*Holds bottle up.*)

Donna (*laughing*) A bloody cheek! C'mon, grab a message bag.

Gil picks up bag of groceries, stuffs Chianti bottle into jacket pocket – Donna makes her way into close and on up the stair.
Gil hefts double-bass off the ground and lurches after Donna.

Gil You know she was stone deaf, don't you? (*Disappearing into close – off.*) Aside from bein' no' well, I mean . . . his maw, yeh? (*Crash of breaking bottle.*) Aw, naw.

Donna (*off*) What was that?

Gil (*off*) No option but to behave yurself now, sweetheart . . .

Enter Paula and Maureen – they look back along street where Dessie and Steeples have got into taxi. Maureen is helping to lug Paula's now enlarged drum kit – each carries several items.

Paula . . . Naw, still canny see it. I mean, he's okay as geetar-vocalists go but . . . naw, canny see it, Mo.

Maureen It's stickin' out a mile, Paula . . . alright, so he's made a mug of himself *and* me getting' mixed up with that Tally cow but that's the result of his mother shufflin' off hur mortal coil an' leavin' hur only son to the mercies of that *evil bitch*.

Paula S'that not a bit strong? No' be better referrin' to hur as a 'durty wee whoor'?

Maureen gives her a 'look'.

Suit yurself. Here, I noticed that Fazzi's huv slashed thur hairstyle prices.

Maureen Yeh . . . apart from a bubble cut.

Paula Don't think I want a bubble cut.

Maureen Just as well . . . they've went *up* in price.

Paula How come?

Maureen The only time I was ever asked for one I made a total arse of it. Customer had to be rushed to the out-patients on the bus . . . off hur work fur three weeks till the worst of the scabs'd healed.

She sets drums down outside salon door – hunts pockets for keys.

The boss gave hur a free voucher for a wig fittin' and a scalp massage but she never ever showed up . . . Some folk don't know when thur well-off, eh?

A light comes on at Dessie's upstairs window – Gil leans out.
    He looks at all the stars in the heavens – takes a deep lungful of night air.

Gil Strange, but I'm gonny miss this dump.

Donna (*leaning out of adjacent window*) Sorry, I was putting the water on for the carbonara . . . did you say something?

Gil Jist wonderin' how yur 'fiancy's' gettin' on.

Donna Me too. Dessie'll be fine, it's that creep Steeples I'm concerned about.

Gil Naw, Eddie's awright . . . okay, so he's a creep but the kinda creep that's been around the music business fur too many years to let wur boy do anythin' stupid, right?

Donna Like what?

Gil I don't know . . . like sharin' his copyright wi' somebody else, fur instance.

Donna In his songs? Like who?

Gil Calm down . . . that was only a 'fur instance', I wasny referrin' to anybody in particular.

Donna Thank God for that, I thought for a moment . . .

Gil I mean, Joey knows fine well that everythin' The Crescents've ever done onstage hus been wrote by . . .

Donna That who's ever done onstage??

Gil The Crescents . . . Dessie not tell you? Him an' me an' Paula an' Joey . . . we . . . are . . . The Crescents!

Donna withdraws from window – unnoticed by Gil.

We wur gonny be 'Underwood Lane and the Darkwood Crescents' but the only one that was prepared to change thur name by deed poll to Underwood Lane was yours truly . . . Ma old man huvvin' been a big fan of Frankie Laine, I couldny see thur was a problem . . . but fur some reason unbeknownst to me, that didny seem to suit everybody so what we had to do was write out aw the words on bitsa paper, cut them up an' put aw the bitsa paper inty a hat an' get wur drummer Paula to stick hur mitt inty the hat an' pull out . . .

Donna appears in the street below pulling on her coat.

. . . Hang on, I thought you wur . . .? Where you off to??

Donna (*buttoning coat*) The Rosebud . . . before that soft mark gets sold down the river.

She sets off along the street as fast as she can manage.

Gil Ho, come back here! What about that carbonara you promised us??

Exit Donna.

Bugger.

Paula appears from salon, a towel round her shoulders – hair in some disarray.

Paula (*calling up to Gil*) 'Scuse me, but could you keep the bloody racket down! Wur tryin' to catch the Top Twenty in here an' what wi' you shoutin' an' bawlin' an' the wonky dryer . . . (*Realising it's Gil.*) Aw God, look who it is, I might've guessed.

Maureen appears from salon.

Maureen Who?

Gil Thought you pair wurny talkin'?

Paula To you? Too right. We wur just about to hear what the Number One record in the country was an' aw we can hear is you *shoutin'*!

Gil Listen, if Eddie Steeples plays his cards right that could be the next Number One record in the country, me *shoutin'*!

Maureen What's he doin' up there?

Paula You deaf? He's shoutin'. (*Shouting up at Gil.*) Well, I wouldny buy it!

37

Maureen Naw, I mean, what's he doin' up there in Dessie's apartment? (*Shouting up at Gil.*) What you doin' up there in Dessie Devlin's apartment when this customer and I have just witnessed him gettin' into a taxi with yur manager not that long back?? (*To Paula.*) D'you think she's up there an' all?

Paula Who, the wee whoor?

Maureen (*shouting up at Gil*) Is *she* up there with you??

Gil Is *who* up here with me??

Maureen (*to Paula*) Can't very well say the 'wee whoor' (*Shouting up at Gil.*) Hur . . . that evil *bitch*!

Gil Hur who??

Maureen *and* **Paula** (*shoutin' up at Gil*) The *Tally cow*!

> *Lights down.*
> *Lights up on Donna wandering you-knows-where, disconsolate. No sign of her quarry (Dessie).*
> *Song: 'Walk Right Back' – Donna lead, with Paula and Maureen.*
> *Enter Dessie at a run – elated – a large envelope clutched in his mitt.*

Dessie Yaaaaaaaaaaaaaaaaaaaaaaaaaaaaaahooooo!!!

> *Lights down.*

SCENE EIGHT

Underwood Lane – one hour later that same evening. No sign of life apart from a glimpse of Maureen all alone inside hairdressing salon. She is putting her coat on for going home.

Dessie (*from afar, off*) Donna?

> *Enter Dessie a few moments later – still elated and slightly squiffier than before but not drunk.*

(*Calling up at window.*) Y'there, sweetheart?

A sleepy-eyed Gil appears at window – leans out.

Gil Who you callin' 'sweetheart'? Away you go before I shout the polis.

Dessie She in bed, yeh? Look. (*Waves envelope.*)

Gil Look what? If you want us to look at somethin' why don't you come up the stair an' we can both . . . (*Penny suddenly dropping – wide awake.*) Stay there . . . jist to get ma shoes on!

Maureen exits salon – starts locking up. Sees Dessie – crosses.

Maureen Hi, Dessie . . . you're a sight fur sore eyes . . . Paula's been regaling me with all yur adventures . . . you and 'Les Croissants' . . . did I tell you I was goin' to night school? That means a French roll, which funnily enough, is also a hairdressing term . . . (*Reaching to touch his unruly mop.*) You must let me do this for you sometime.

Dessie Hang off, ma hair's fine.

Maureen No, it isn't . . . it's gorgeous. (*Biting her glove.*) D'you want me to . . . (*Stops biting glove.*) d'you want me to post that for you?

She reaches for big envelope.

Dessie (*swiping it out of reach*) Uh-uh! You know what's in here, don't you?

Maureen Now, how would I possibly know that? (*Leaning closer.*) Yur such a tease, Dessie Devlin.

Gil appears in the street – he is wearing one shoe.

Gil So you ur . . . c'mon, give's a look.

He elbows Maureen aside and takes hold of the big envelope.

Maureen Oooow! Watch it, you!

Dessie Jist huv to read the furst paragraph.

He leans in close as Gil takes a piece of paper out.

Gil Chuck crowdin' us well!

Dessie I want to see yur face . . .

Gil's eyes open wide as he silently mouths the words of the first few lines to himself – he looks at Dessie – stunned.

. . . There, I told you!

Gil A record . . . wur gonny make a record!

He grabs hold of Maureen and starts jumping up and down – laughing and yahooing.

Maureen (*stony-faced throughout – to Dessie*) Gonny tell him to hang off!

Instead of going to her rescue Dessie joins in – Maureen now sandwiched between Dessie and Gil as they laugh and bounce.
    Enter Donna looking ill – Dessie and Gil keep on bouncing the unfortunate and unwilling Maureen up and down for some little longer until Dessie finally spots Donna – breaks off.

Dessie Donna . . . where've you been? I thought you wur up the stair asleep!

He rushes towards her – she stumbles into his arms.

Donna I couldn't get a taxi so I walked . . .

Dessie Your walkin' days are over, sweetheart. Ho, Gil, let hur see that bitta paper!

Donna By the time I got there you were gone . . . oh, God.

Dessie Here . . . this'll cheer you up.

*Gil hands 'contract' to Dessie – Dessie holds it up for
Donna*

Donna (*weakly*) I haven't got my glasses . . . you read it
to me.

Dessie Naw, you . . . I want to see yur reaction. (*To Gil and
Maureen.*) Wait . . . wait . . .

*Donna casts an eye over the printed page – taking longer
than expected.*

Gil Why don't you jist tell hur?

Dessie . . . Wait . . . wait!

Donna (*explosively*) You *imbecile*!

*She shoves Dessie away from her with all her might –
Dessie staggers back – bewildered.*

Dessie (*casting around*) Who?? Where??

Donna Have you read this??

Dessie I hud a glance at it, yeh.

Gil It says wuv to make a record.

Donna (*overlapping*) Shuttup! Let me actually read it to
you, Des. '. . . as to the material that shall constitute said
recordings . . .'

Gil See? Told you.

Maureen Shuttup.

Donna '. . . hereinafter referred to as "the songs" . . . four
of "the songs" having already been submitted and approved
– the credit to read: Music and Lyrics by Desmond
Devlin . . .'

Dessie There you go . . . hunky-dory . . . (*Reaching hand
out.*) Give us that t'we get it framed.

Donna '. . . and Joseph Diamond . . .'

Dessie What?

Gil (*aside*) Bugger.

Donna '. . . *and* J. Edward Steeples . . .'

Dessie, Maureen *and* **Gil** What??

Donna I thought you were meant to be halfway smart, Dessie?? How could you let this happen to us!

Dessie (*sobering up*) C'mon, doll, could happen to anybody . . . Let's you an' me put wur heads together an' see if we canny . . .

Donna I'm not talking about you and me, you moron! I'm talking about me and this baby!

Dessie Aw, fur Christ's sake! If I hear you mention you an' this . . . this *baby* one more time I'll . . . Don't turn yur back on me! This's ma life wur talkin' about here . . . my *life*! If you don't like it then you and yur baby can bugger off!!

He grabs Gil's arm and starts hauling him away.

Gil (*trying to get free*) Hang off! What you doin?? Get offy us! (*Exeunt.*)

Dessie (*off*) I want a word wi' you, Diamond! An' wi' you, Steeples!

Donna sinks to her knees and sobs – Maureen watches Dessie and Gil disappear.
Fazzi, hitherto unnoticed inside café, removes 'For Sale' sign from the window and replaces it with a sign saying 'SOLD'.
Maureen comes to her senses and helps Donna to her feet. Fazzi comes out of the café into the street – Maureen supports Donna as they stumble towards the café.
Father and daughter confront one another – Fazzi appears to be unmoved. After a few moments Fazzi

opens his arms wide – Donna moves forward and falls into her father's arms. Fazzi gathers his distressed child in his arms and they disappear into the café.

Maureen bends and picks up scarf that Dessie has given Donna and raises it to her lips.

Song: 'You Don't Know' – Maureen, lead, with band and BVs, off.

Interval.

Act Two

SCENE ONE

Song: 'A White Sports Coat' – ensemble.

Lights up on Underwood Lane, eighteen months later. The café now transformed into Eddie's Nite Club and Grill and the hairdressing salon now calling itself Bubble Cuts.

Dessie enters – homesick and jaded . . . dumps guitar case and holdall. He is wearing an 'Italianate' suit (short jacket, shorter hair, winklepickers) – does some ostentatious rubber-necking, like he's never been in this neighbourhood before.

Frankie appears at door of club – holds door open as Dessie draws near . . . Dessie keeps on prowling.

Frankie Ho! This door's a ton weight!

Dessie (*giving joint the once-over*) Canny believe this used to be Bruno's . . .

Frankie You comin' in or you no' comin' in??

Dessie (*peering inside*) what happened to the café?

Frankie Never you heed what happened . . . you a member?

Dessie 'Member'?

Frankie Aye . . . a *member*?

Dessie Used to be a member of Our Lady of the Seven Dolours Boys' Club, if that's any help?

Frankie Hang on . . . I know your face from somewhere . . . naw, don't tell us . . .

Dessie Wasny goin' to.

Frankie Yur no' a pal of Paula's, by any chance?

44

Dessie What's that . . . like a 'Friend of Dorothy's'? (*Backing away.*) Sorry, didny realise you wur that kinda 'club'.

Frankie Huh?

Gil appears at window upstairs

Gil Ho!

Dessie (*to Frankie*) Did you jist hear a '*Ho!*'?

Frankie Here a *ho*, there a *ho*, everywhere a *ho*, *ho* . . . lemme huv a look-see.

Steps outside – spots Gil at window.

Was that *you* shoutin'??

Gil Aye . . . how was London??

Frankie I huvny been to London.

Gil No' you . . . *him*! Be right down, Des. (*Disappears from view.*)

Frankie Did he jist cry you 'Des'?

Dessie Who, me? Don't think so . . . the name's Dorbie . . . Dorbie Henderson . . . and you are?

Frankie Yur no' the same Dorbie Henderson that used to be Dessie Whatsisname? Cos I've been waitin' fur the last eighteen months to catch up wi' him.

Gil reappears at window.

Gil Jist to find a paira troosers!

Disappears again – Maureen appears from Bubble Cuts hairdressing salon – unrecognisably glamorous now. Spots Dessie.

Maureen *Aaaaaaaaaaaaaaaaaargh!!*

Takes a run at Dessie – throws her arms around him and kisses him fiercely – holds kiss – finally breaks away.

So . . . how was London??

Dessie (*reeling away*) London was . . . (*Fingering his lips.*) London was . . . Huv we *met*??

Maureen (*laughing*) Listen to him . . . he's every bit as hilarious as he was when he left here five hundred an' forty seven days, ten hours, an' seventeen minutes ago . . . It's *me* . . . Mo!!

Dessie Mo *who*?? Only Mo I ever came across was a total *dog*.

Maureen (*tickled*) God, yur just as funny as ever . . . funnier even!

A stony-faced Dessie exchanges looks with stony-faced Frankie. Frankie shrugs.

Did you get any the letters I wrote you?

Dessie *What* letters?

Maureen I wrote to you three times a week an' twice on a Saturday, sent them off to 'Dessie Devlin, care of Parlophone Records' . . .

Frankie (*galvanised*) See?? You ur so him!

Maureen . . . I even put stamps on some of them.

Frankie (*to Dessie*) What'd you go an' say you wurny fur??

Dessie Listen, if it's about that amplifier you lent us, I can let you huv an address in Pentonville where you can go pick it up . . . (*To Maureen.*) Wish you'd thought to send a snapshot along wi' yur letters, I might've . . .

Gil appears. Dessie shoves guitar bag at Frankie to hold.

. . . Gilfedder!!

They stumble towards one another – looks like they might embrace but, fortunately, Gil has to pause and pull his braces up over his shoulders.

Maureen (*to Frankie*) Allow me.

Takes guitar bag and clasps it tightly to her.

Gil Yuv hudda haircut!

Dessie Where? (*Runs hand over his head.*) Aw, so I have.

Gil So, how was the Big Smoke? Where was it you wur again?

Dessie Where was it I wasny?? Archway wi' ma Uncle Hughie . . . Vauxhall when I got flang outta Archway . . . Norwood wi' a coupla guys from Largs I met up wi' in Hounslow wi' a guy I met in Norwood that'd never heard of Largs, never heed been there . . . then Clerkenwell with a coupla Art students . . . Harlesden when I was totally on ma uppers . . . Islington when I got back on ma feet . . . finished up in Tooting in a hostel fur the handicapped . . . (*Casting around.*) Lotta changes around here, eh?

Frankie (*takes dog-eared envelope from pocket*) Ho . . . Eddie Steeples asked me to give you this if I ever bumped inty you which I now huv, so there you go . . . (*Hands envelope to Dessie.*) Mission accomplished.

Dessie glances at envelope – pockets it. Frankie disappears into club.

Dessie (*to Gil*) You still servin' yur time wi' what was it we cried wurselves again . . . The Cresents, yeh?

Gil Hud a big pow-wow when you done yur disappearin' act . . . came off the road fur three month . . . brung in new personnel . . . Eddie swapped me onty rhythm guitar . . . me an' Joey wrote some new numbers . . . done a demo disc, hopin' fur some radio plays. S'matter of fact, wur booked to launch some new material here the night.

Dessie Where's 'here' . . . in the street?

Gil Naw, in there.

Dessie Where . . . Fatso's café?

Gil Eddie's Nite Club.

Dessie Not goin' to squeeze too many punters inty that joint, Gilbert. What's the seatin' capacity . . . about a dozen max, yeh?

Gil It's actually about four hunner.

Dessie Four hunner?? You been smokin' what-d'you-cry-it . . . marry-joo-wanna?

Maureen He's right enough, Des . . . Steeples bought up the Boys' Club premises at the back of the café and got the workmen to knock through . . . you want to see the size of the place now . . . What's it like, Gilbert?

Dessie (*amused*) Better get maself a ticket quick then. (*To Gil.*) Who is it I'm going to see again?

Gil Boy's jist puttin' the poster up.

Dessie turns to look – Frankie slips poster into display case. It reads: 'For One Nite Only "DONATELLA AND THE DIAMONDS" Prior to North American Tour'. Dessie's jaw drops – he turns to look at Gil in disbelief – Frankie slaps a 'SOLD OUT' sticker across poster as Dessie turns back round to see if his eyes have deceived him or not – further incredulity.

Maureen You can come on ma ticket, Des . . . I got maself a 'twofur' just in case Paula wanted to come before I realised she'd already be there in the band. (*Gives a little laugh at her naivety.*)

Gil Here, I better blow . . . get changed inty ma stage clobber . . . (*Moving off – stops.*) If yur postcard hud came earlier I could've saved you a bed, Dessie, but wuv got a busloada cousins comin' from West Kilbride fur the show. Catch up wi' you later, yeh?

Exit Gil. As he disappears, Maureen moves relentlessly in on Dessie.

Maureen Thur's always my place . . .

Dessie (*still in daze*) Your place?

Maureen . . . I've just moved in over the salon, it's really quite cosy.

Dessie Aw, yeh . . . sure . . . that would be . . . er . . . thanks, doll.

Maureen Lemme go and make up a bed for you . . . (*Picks up Dessie's holdall.*) Make sure I've got that ticket. And I'll keep this in ma room . . . (*Holds up guitar bag.*) Just in case you get yur juices flowin' during the night and want to produce something truly monumental . . . (*Trips.*) Bugger! (*Shoves salon door open with her foot.*) Wish you'd got all them letters I sent you.

Disappears inside – Dessie comes out of daze. Takes dog-eared envelope from pocket and tears it open.
Song: 'Put Your Head On My Shoulder' – Maureen and ensemble.

SCENE TWO

Tight spot on Frankie at the mic.

Frankie Good evenin', ladies'n'gents . . . welcome to Eddie's Nite Club . . . could youse put yur hands together fur a buncha guys'n'gals' final farewell appearance afore gettin' onty a plane an' takin' the US of A by the baw hairs an' doin' thur nappers in . . . here, live, an' rarin' to go . . . Donnatella and The Diamonds!

Lights up on the band – Paula on drums, Gil on rhythm guitar, Joey on lead guitar, and Donna, looking terrific with a bass guitar at her hip, launch straight into their opening song: 'Will You Still Love Me Tomorrow'.

Lights down on band – lights up on Maureen and Dessie – Maureen dolled up to the nines, Dessie pacing to and fro.

Maureen I would be just as happy goin' to see a movie.

Dessie Quit rushing us, it's been two bloody years!

Maureen Correction . . . five hundred an' forty seven days, *seventeen* hours an' . . .

Dessie Okay, *okay*!! It's still a bloody long time! What if she's brung the kid with hur??

Lights off – lights up on club. Donna paces nervously to and fro while Joey sits with his feet up during the interval.

Joey C'mon, doll, relax . . . he never showed up fur the furst half . . .

Donna . . . He could easily turn up after the interval . . . how do I break it to him?

Joey Tell him the truth . . . (*Catches hold of her wrist.*) that you found me *irresistible*. (*Pulls her onto his lap.*)

Donna Not about *us*. About . . . *ahya, bugger!*

Joey kisses her greedily – Donna struggles before giving up and returning the kiss in spades.

Lights up on club – Donnatella and The Diamonds have just finished their set to great applause and cheers. A mix of 'whoops' and 'bravos' from audience as Dessie, coat pulled up over his head, is guided by Maureen to a front row seat which he sinks down into.

Gil (*into mic*) Thank you . . . thank you very much . . . you've been a terrific audience . . .

More cheers and whistles, etc.

. . . so great, in fact, that I'd like to introduce you to somebody that's here the night . . . somebody you should all know . . . journeyed all the way here from London last night to make sure he'd be in time to catch the show this evening . . .

Dessie sinks lower in his seat.

Maureen C'mon, Dessie . . . buck up . . . wur goin' to meet somebody from London!

Gil . . . an old friend of ours and a former *founding* member of 'The Darkwood Crescents' . . .

Cheers – whistles and foot stomping.

. . . on yur feet, Dessie . . . where is he?

Spotlight ranges around trying to locate Dessie.

Maureen (*jumping to her feet*) He's here! (*To Dessie, now on floor.*) I never twigged it was *you*! Quick! (*Standing up.*) Here . . . over here!

Spotlight swings around and lands on Maureen – Dessie is now on the floor. Maureen hauls him to his feet and lets the spotlight pick him out. Cheers and applause from all and sundry.

Dessie (*to Maureen through clenched teeth*) I'm gunny swing fur you!

Gil I'd like to invite Des up to join us by way of an encore . . . Dessie Devlin, ladies an' gentlemen!

Huge round of applause.
    Despite Dessie's protestations, Maureen gets behind him and propels him towards the stage – Gil reaches a hand out, hauls Dessie onstage and hands him a guitar while Donna is forcibly prevented from quitting the stage by Joey. Dessie turns to Paula behind drum kit and

counts her in while Joey weighs in with guitar intro –
Dessie leans into mic.

    Song: 'Unchained Melody', 'Bye Bye Lover' or 'You've
Lost That Lovin' Feelin'' – Dessie with band.

    Thunderous applause greets Dessie's contribution.

    Joey, Gil and Paula stand to take their 'curtain call' –
Dessie grabs Donna's arm to prevent her quitting the
stage.

Dessie I only just got yur note . . .

Donna Yeh, Frankie said. I lost it, Des.

Dessie . . . Well, Eddie must've found it, stuck it in an
envelope, passed it onty Frankie who passed it onty me.
From the labour ward, that one, yeh?

Donna No, you don't understand . . .

Dessie I do so understand! I never had an address fur you
to send it to . . . you wur about to have . . .

Donna . . . the baby, yeh.

Dessie *Our* baby . . . so, what was it, a boy or a girl?

Donna A wee girl . . .

Dessie (*thrilled*) *Naw!* I bet you she was *adorable*!

Donna She was.

Dessie Told you!

Donna Four month premature . . . she died in my arms.

Dessie What?? (*Lets go of her arm.*)

Donna I lost our beautiful wee baby . . . I'm so sorry.

    She turns on her heel and hurries offstage – disappears
into the darkness, leaving Dessie poleaxed.

    Gil retrieves guitar from Dessie and hands it to
Frankie who has reverted to being their roadie.

Gil God, that took us back. It was probably on this very spot . . . right here. Christ, that's when we furst met up wi' Eddie Steeples . . . d'you mind Donna's old man Fatso comin' beltin' down the stair an' readin' the riot act? That's when you an' hur . . . (*Twigging that something is up.*) you awright, Dessie?

Paula comes up behind Gil and wraps her arms around him.

Paula Hi, lover boy . . . d'you want to buy me a *cock*-tail?

Gil Dessie . . . ?

A low throaty growl as Paula nuzzles Gil's neck.

(*To Dessie.*) If you fancy goin' furra pint, I'm yur man . . . (*Giggling – to Paula.*) Gerroff us! Ooooow . . . chuck it!

Maureen appears.

Maureen C'mon, you pair . . . behave yurselfs . . . that is disgustin' . . . (*To Dessie.*) So, did she break it to you?

Dessie What? Aw . . . er . . . yeh, she . . . er . . .

Maureen I mean, I would've told you but it didny feel right somehow . . .

Dessie . . . Naw, sure.

Maureen . . . He's been showin' off all over the place.

Dessie Who . . . Gilfedder? I'm not surprised, it's no' like he's ever hudda girlfriend, never heed one like . . . (*Stops short.*) Hang on, if he's winchin' hur, then who is it that Joey . . . ?

Maureen That's who I'm talkin' about about . . . *Joey* and . . . hang on, I thought you just said that she'd broke the news to you about hur and . . . ?

Dessie What?? You mean . . . ?

Maureen . . . Joey and yur ex . . . they got *spliced* at the Registry Office in Gilmour Street last Tuesday.

Lights down.

SCENE THREE

A confessional box in the church of Our Lady of the Seven Dolours – Father Durcan in his half of the box, nodding off.
   Enter Dessie. He crosses to box – goes inside and kneels down.

Dessie (*crossing himself*) Bless me, Father, for I have . . . (*Hesitates.*)

Father Durcan (*drawing himself together*) I suggest the word you're groping for is 'sinned', Desmond . . . how long is it since your last confession?

Dessie Aw . . . er . . . lemme think . . . must be about nine or ten . . . er . . .

Father Durcan Weeks? Months?

Dessie . . . Naw, *years* . . . must be about ten years, Father . . . or mebbe it's mebbe closer to eight . . . eight or nine . . .

Father Durcan C'mon, Dessie, stop fuckin' about, you didn't come here to make yur confession, you came here because you find yurself in a hole . . . a great, black uncomfortable hole and you want a bit of help to claw yur way back out into the sunlight . . . isn't that it?

Dessie Yeh, sort of. Did you jist say *'fuckin''*?

Father Durcan What d'you mean, 'sort of'?? You either do want a bit of help or you don't . . . C'mon, get a move on, I'm desperate for a smoke.

Dessie Awright . . . I do.

Father Durcan Okay, here's my advice . . . Stop arsin' about feelin' sorry for yurself . . . you done the durty on the Fazzi girl by promisin' to tie the knot, then getting' hur up the duff before chuckin' hur over an' beatin' it to London . . . you know she lost the child, don't you? Did you try and comfort hur in any way? Did you convey to her how sorry you were?

Dessie I never even knew till last night that she had lost the . . .

Father Durcan (*overlapping*) Now, there's somethin' that Hart's Christian Doctrine describes as an 'act of reparation', which means, in essence . . .

Dessie . . . 'to make amends in some way commensurate with the harm or injury inflicted upon another person' . . . Yeh, yeh, we all know what 'repartation' means.

Father Durcan Good! So you can stop playin' 'Mr Wiseguy' and get crackin' on it! (*Coming round to confront Dessie.*) And if I hear tell that you've failed in this particular 'act of reparation', I'll personally kick the fuckin' daylights out of you, d'you hear me??

Genuflects to altar and crosses himself – produces packet of Gold Flake from under his cassock.

And you can save the cursin' and swearin' fur the pub . . . Yur poor old mother that's out the back there'll be turnin' in her grave, so she will.

Jams unlit cigarette in his mouth – stalks off.

Fuckin' heathen . . .

Pauses to light his cigarette from votive candle – and exits. Dessie gets up to leave as Donna enters. She crosses herself, eyes closed.
Song: 'I've Been Loving You Too Long' – Paula and band, off.

*Donna gets up – crosses herself and leaves – Dessie
watcher her go.*
Lights down.

SCENE FOUR

*Eddie Steeples' office – the following day. Two chairs and
desk. Variety of rock'n'roll memorabilia.*
Dessie stands with his back to the door – enter Steeples.

Steeples So . . . long time, no see, Dessie. (*Removes overcoat.*)

Dessie Get to the nub, Eddie . . . not in the mood fur
banter . . .

Steeples drapes overcoat over the chair – sits.

Steeples Just after wavin' the *quartette* off at Canal Street
railway station . . . Park yur rump.

Dessie Didny realise you could get a train all the way to the
States . . . (*Sits.*)

Steeples They urny goin' to the States, thur off to North
America . . . train gets them to Troon, taxi takes them to the
aerodrome . . . flight ferries them to Toronto, then it's a
Greyhound bus to Calgary, Winnipeg, then Niagara
Falls . . . finish up wi' five nights at the Buddies Club,
Medicine Lake Reservation, Manitoba, an' I hud to pull a
few strings jist to get them that . . . huvny got the right
material fur the States as yet . . . which is where you come
in. I'm talkin' . . . original songs wi' a sublte Yankee
bias . . . geddit?

Dessie How's about you an' Joey knockin' out some
'original' songs wi' a subtle Yankee bias'? After all, you an'
him wur credited on wur furst album . . .

Steeples C'mon, Des, I explained that mix-up at the
time . . . Joey an' me wur as flabbergasted as you wur. In

fact, I don't know if you're aware of this but I done ma own investigatin' an' you know what?

Dessie Yeh . . . it was you an' Joey's idea all along except youse got rumbled . . . Let's put it down to 'amnesia' an' furget about it, Eddie.

Steeples Mother's life, Dessie . . . it was this barrister boy in Brixton the record company had brung in . . . he only hud partial hearin' in the one ear . . . me an' him wur never off the phone to one another, hence the bungle wi' yur copyright, know what I'm sayin'? I was fur huvvin' the bastart castrated but all they done was send him to the Ear, Nose an' Throat hospital in Harley Street that I hud to shell out fur. Jeeezus. (*Pause.*) So, what do you think?

Dessie I think yur a lyin' bastart, Eddie.

Steeples (*leaning across desk*) I just huv to dial a number an' I can huv you shot fur sayin' stuff like that. (*Sitting back.*) I wasny talkin' about the barrister boy, I was askin' you what you thought about joinin' The Diamonds? I can shunt Gilfedder back onty bass fiddle, get Joey a Les Paul wi' a bigger amp, an' shift what-d'you-cry-hur . . . your ex, his missus . . . onty keyboards, let you come in on vocals an' acoustic . . . write yurself an' hur a buncha songs, Stateside Tour guaranteed . . . (*Leaning across desk.*) plus a record deal fur *real*, this time . . . bona fide credits fur yur songs, exceptin' this time around . . . an' I don't want this broadcast outside of this office . . . wi' an American *major*, the Vice President of which hud a listen to thon tape I sent off to that buncha bandits in London that buggered yur songs, copyright up by passin' it onty that bastard barrister boy from Brixton an' you know what he said . . . ?

Dessie Who? The bastard barrister boy from Brixton?

Steeples . . . *Naw*, the *Vice President*! On that telephone there . . . long-distance call from Burbank, California! Know what he said?

Dessie Shove it, Eddie.

Steeples Naw . . . he said . . .

Dessie stands up.

. . . where you off to??

Dessie Somewhere I can breathe right . . . air in here's *foul.*

Exit Dessie.
Lights to black.

Steeples (*from blackout*) I can huv you shot, jist remember that!

Song: 'Singing the Blues' – Gil.

SCENE FIVE

Underwood Lane – ten days later. Night going into the wee small hours. The neon lettering on Eddie's Nite Club glows luridly red against the blackness of the night – a harsh white 'OPEN' winks on and off in the club window. All around the blacked-out tenements loom – the tawdry 'watering-hole' becomes an alluring oasis in the otherwise hellish darkness.

Just inside the door of the club, Frankie keeps an eye out for members, allowing them in or out as it pleases him.

Enter Dessie at far end of street – a lonely and dejected figure, hands thrust deep in pockets, hair dishevelled.

The 'OPEN' sign on the club flickers and goes out – sundry groups of members spill out and make their unsteady way home.

Dessie stands with his back to the building, hands in pockets – lost. He sets light to a dog-end.

Sound of muffled voices raised in anger – scuffling and thumps – Dessie couldn't care less. The door to the club is thrown open – Fazzi, practically unrecognisable in scruffy overcoat and the worse for wear, is pitched headlong into the street – he stumbles forward and lands heavily nearby Dessie, who couldn't give a toss.

Frankie (*ripping up Fazzi's membership card*) Consider yur membership from here on . . . *void*! No' worth the pasteboard it's printed on . . . *right*??

He scatters the 'confetti' into the street and slams the club door. Dessie tilts his head back and sends a spiral of smoke curling into the night air.
    Club door is flung open again – Frankie chucks Fazzi's hat at him.

And if I catch you pesterin' Mr Steeples fur money again, you're furra right doin', get me?

Slams door shut – Fazzi, dazed . . . makes an attempt to stand upright.

(*Feebly.*) Cazza Madonna . . .

Dessie chokes on fag-end – turns to look at Fazzi, now on his hands and knees.

Dessie Good God . . . *Fatso*!

Drops fag-end and tries to get Fazzi onto his pins again. Fazzi sways – his legs buckle. Dessie grasps him under the arms . . . supports him. A roll of thunder.

(*Looking up at sky.*) Aye, awright, I get it! (*Loudly.*) Ho! Y'there, Mo??

Fazzi (*groggy*) 'E . . . who are you? (*Feeling bare head.*) Whatta you do wid ma facking '*at*??

Dessie (*in direction of Bubble Cuts*) It's an *emergency* . . . wake up!!

Fazzi I am awake up . . . don' 'ave to shout ma facking ears affa ma heid!

Dessie *Maureeeeeeeeeeeen!!*

*A light snaps on over the hairdressing salon – Dessie
bends to pick up Fazzi's hat.*
Maureen appears at lighted window – peers out.

Maureen Good grief . . . Mr Fazzi! What you doin' down
there at this time of night?? I thought you wur . . .

Dessie stands up.

Aaaaaaargh! Who's that with you??

Dessie It's me . . . Dessie . . . let us in, Mo, he's in a bit of a
state.

Maureen What you up to? I thought you couldny stand him?

Dessie Jist let us in, eh?

*Maureen disappears from window – lights go on
downstairs – Maureen holds door open.*

(*Cramming hat onto Fazzi's head.*) C'mon . . . one foot in
front of the other . . . there you go.

*They stumble towards the lighted doorway.
Lights down.*

SCENE SIX

Song: 'I Fall to Pieces'.
*Lights up on Donna, Gil, Paula and Joey just arrived
back from their North American Tour, exhausted and
disgruntled – big pile of luggage, flight cases et al waiting at
the taxi rank.*
*Gil has a noodle on guitar – Donna starts to hum the
opening bars of 'Can I Have My Money Back' – the others
join in, one by one, until it becomes a jaundiced, no-holds-
barred condemnation of their cynical management's
crooked and deceitful handling of their 'stateside' tour.*
Headlight beams – Donna sticks a hand up.

Donna Taxi!

Fazzi sits back in barber's chair in Bubble Cuts while Maureen lathers his chin with shaving cream. Dessie is at the door, looking out onto the street. Maureen gets a cut-throat razor from drawer – holds it at arm's length, a terrified look on her face and walks gingerly towards Dessie. A snore from Fazzi in the chair.

Maureen (*holding razor out – to Dessie*) Here . . . d'you want to do it?

Dessie Me? That's the same razor the bugger nicked his own ear with when he threatened me wi' it . . . *You* do it.

Maureen C'mon, we can't let him go back to wherever it is he's stayin' lookin' like a *hobo* . . . here, take it!

She thrusts it towards Dessie – Dessie snatches it from her.

Dessie (*like he's cut himself*) Waaaaaaah!

Maureen Aw, my God!

Dessie I was only kiddin'.

Maureen See you, Dessie Devlin! (*Gives him a dunt.*)

Dessie Ahyah!

Fazzi wakes up with a start – looks around him.

Fazzi 'E?? Where I am??

Dessie Relax, yur in safe hands . . . (*Holding up razor.*) Jist gonny cut yur gizzard.

Fazzi lurches from the chair.

Fazzi Eddie Steeple . . . 'e send you frighten me cos he still owe me fifteen hunner quids furra ma café . . . (*Loudly.*) 'Elp! Aiuto!! Polizia!!

Moving unsteadily towards the door – clutches at hairdryer.

Maureen C'mon, Mr Fazzi, nobody's goin' to hurt you . . . it's *me* . . . Maureen . . . Mo . . . *Marina*, yeh?

Fazzi You no' Marina . . . Marina . . . *brutta* . . . like a *dog* . . . si?

Maureen (*to Dessie*) Not quite so comical when he says it.

Dessie D'you think that was true?

Maureen What . . . the '*dog*' terminology?

Dessie Naw . . . about Steeples owin' him that much dough fur his premises?

A low-voltage spark from hairdryer Fazzi is clutching – he keels over unnoticed.

Maureen I wouldny be all that surprised.

Dessie Frankie boy said somethin' about if didny chuck annoyin' Eddie about money, he was gonny . . .

Maureen (*spotting Fazzi on floor*) Aw, my God!

Dessie . . . Stand back, doll.

They rush across to Fazzi's side, Dessie's arm outstretched to prevent Maureen getting to close. Dessie crouches over.

(*Loudly.*) D'you want this shave or d'you not want this shave??

Song: 'It Doesn't Matter Anymore' – Dessie and Donna in and out of dialogue.

Church of Our Lady of the Seven Dolours – evening, two days later. Fazzi's coffin sits on its bier before the high altar. Donna, wearing black veil, kneels in a nearby pew next to it . . . bows her head.

Dessie enters – comes and sits in the pew across from her. A lengthy silence before he speaks.

Dessie So, how was the North American Tour?

Donna (*head still bowed*) Hellish.

Silence.

Dessie Had a meetin' wi' Eddie while you were away.

Another silence.

Made us an offer to write some new stuff an' join up wi' you an' Gil and Paula and . . . whatsisname . . . oh, congratulations, by the way, on yur . . . er . . .

Donna (*head still bowed*) Thanks.

Another silence.

Dessie I'm seriously thinkin' about it.

Donna The offer, yeh?

Crosses herself and sits upright, looking straight ahead.

Dessie I'm also thinkin' about the other matter but I don't suppose I can do very much about that now, is there?

Donna Not a lot, no.

Dessie Tell me somethin' . . . did that response . . . that barbed and witty *comeback* in married love's defence come straight from the heart . . . or is it just me?

Lights down.

SCENE NINE

Eddie Steeples' office – later, same day (Fazzi's funeral).
Steeples seated behind desk – Joey standing, facing away.

Joey You did what??

Swings round to face Steeples.

Steeples I done it fur you an' The Diamonds . . . gave him an ultimatum.

Joey Like what . . . if he didny accept yur offer you'd cancel his Club Membership?

Steeples S'far as I'm aware, he husny got Club Membership . . . Naw, told him I could huv him shot.

Joey Aw, that's just dandy . . . 'Write them a coupla hit numbers or you'll find yurself in somebody's coal bunker wi' a coupla slugs in yur noggin'?

Steeples Don't recollect any mention of 'coal bunkers', Joey . . . anyhow, he's thinkin' it over . . . hud a phonecall this mornin' before they went to the funeral.

Joey Before *who* went to the funeral?

Steeples Dessie'n'Donna . . . What's up you're no' there?

Joey Don't worry . . . I'm goin' to be . . . (*Crossing to door.*) I'll huv a word wi' *you* later!

Lights down.

Fazzi's graveside – Dessie, Donna, Paula, Gil and Maureen
are among the mourners. Donna veiled and all in black,
Paula in black T-shirt with skull and crossbones motif plus
dark glasses, Gil also wearing shades while Maureen is in
all-black outfit.
Father Durcan is concluding the ceremony by sprinkling
holy water whilst intoning prayers for the dead in Latin,
concluding with . . .

Father Durcan . . . ashes to ashes . . . dust to dust . . .
(*Crossing himself.*) and may the Lord have mercy on his soul.

Ragged responses of 'Amen'. Father Durcan turns to have
a word with some mourners. Dessie, Donna, Paula, Gil
and Maureen all light up cigarettes – a collective
exhalation of relief.

Dessie (*to Donna*) You've met ma landlady, haven't you?

Maureen Yeh, we know each other to look to . . . (*To*
Donna.) Don't listen to him, we're just very close
friends . . . aren't we, Dessie?

Donna Yeh, I remember you mentioning that at the last
funeral.

Paula (*to Donna*) Me an' Gilbert here want to convey
wur . . . er . . . (*To Gil.*) What was it again?

Gil Wur condolences.

Paula . . . Yeh . . . wur *condolences*. (*To Donna.*) You must
be dead cut up, yeh?

Donna At least nobody hurled themselves into the grave
this time around. Thanks, Paula.

Gil S'up Joey's no' here?

Dessie Canny say I blame him. I didny want to come maself.

Gil You didny come yurself, you came wi' Donna there.

Paula (*to Donna*) So who was it hurled thurselves inty the grave the last time round?? Wasny the old bag's that hud cancer, was it?

Donna No, it was Papa . . . at my mum's funeral. I was twelve at the time.

Paula God, that's dead romantic . . . (*To Gil.*) Trust you're gonny do the same at mines? (*Gives him a nudge.*)

Gil Aw, thanks a bunch, you jist knocked the fag outta ma mitt!

Father Durcan crosses – spots Dessie.

Father Durcan Good morning, Desmond . . . I didn't see you at mass but I see you're crackin' on with the *reparation* work . . .

Gil retrieves his fag-end.

Ah, good man, Gilbert . . . (*Lights own cigarette from Gil's.*) I don't think I know the young lady in the 'pirate outfit'.

Gil (*retrieving own cigarette*) This's Paula . . . hur an' I's winchin', Father.

Father Durcan Oh . . . and what parish are you from, *Pauline*?

Paula The Orange Lodge in Castle Street . . . an' this isny a 'pirate outfit' . . . it was bought furra friend's wedding . . . she was marryin' a *Catholic*. C'mon, *you*.

She links arms with Gil and drags him off – Enter Joey.

Dessie (*to Donna*) Oh-oh . . . don't look now but yur 'kid-on' hubbie's just arrived.

Donna Where? (*Turning to look.*) God, so he has . . . (*To Dessie.*) What d'you mean, '*kid-on*' husband?

Joey mops his brow – having rushed to get there.

Joey Don't tell me I've missed the bugger??

Dessie I'm sure if you asked the boy wi' the shovel nicely, he would dig him back up so you could say 'arrivadeci' to him . . .

Starts to move off.

Joey Ho! Get back here, it's *you* I want to see!

Dessie stops – turns.

Dessie Me?

Joey (*to Donna*) No disrespect to yur old man, sweetheart, but this canny wait . . . (*To Dessie as he approaches.*) Aye, *you*. I'm jist after seein' Eddie about that business youse two wur discussin' this mornin', and you know what?

Dessie (*exchanging glances with Donna*) About his *offer*, yeh?

Joey Over *ma* dead body, *right*!

Lights down.

SCENE ELEVEN

Underwood Lane – evening of the day of Fazzi's funeral – Frankie at his post of bouncer outside Eddie's Nite Club.
Enter Dessie at end of street with Maureen trailing after.
Frankie inches door open and gives a whistle – Steeples appears and waits for Dessie and Maureen to draw closer.

Steeples So, how'd yur funeral go?

Dessie Wasny *ma* funeral, it was Bruno Fazzi's funeral.

Steeples D'you see Joey there?

Maureen Ye, he was talkin' to Dessie here.

Steeples That's who I'm talkin' to, doll . . . clam up . . . (*To Dessie.*) So, how did it go?

67

Dessie Aw, you know . . . Priest said a few words, scattered a handfulla durt'n'chuckies over the box, trousered a coupla quid . . . box was lowered inty the abyss, then it was off to the Café Riche above La Scala furra purvey an' a few jars, then back to the Chapel House furra . . .

Steeples (*butting in*) Yur *conversation* wi' *Joey* I'm *talkin'*!!

Dessie acts 'the dunce' while Steeples holds Frankie back.

Dessie Aw, that? Wasny much of a 'conversation' . . . he said 'Don't tell me I've missed the bugger?' and I said 'I'm sure if you asked him nicely, the boy wi' the shovel . . . '

Steeples releases Frankie, who grabs Dessie by the lapels.

Aaaaaaaaya!!

Maureen (*laughs – to Dessie*) He wasny goin' to have him dug up?? That is hilarious! (*To Steeples.*) Don't *you* think it's hilarious? Wonder what he'd've looked like??

Frankie Bit like you're gonny look like if you don't chuck actin' the goat an' let Mr Steeples an' the boy here get on wi' thur business meetin'!

Maureen Get *you*!! Never realised this was a '*business* meeting'?? D'you want me to go?

Steeples, Dessie *and* **Frankie** Aye!

Maureen (*rattled*) Aw. *Right.*

Maureen turns on her heel and makes her way across to the salon.

Right!! (*Over shoulder – to Dessie.*) And don't you come bangin' on ma bedroom door durin' the night . . . A herd of stampedin' horses on thur hunkers wouldny get me up to answer it!

Rattling of keys and muttered curses as she opens salon door and disappears inside – noise of crashing furniture

et al. Steeples, Frankie and Dessie look at one another –
Frankie releases Dessie.

Steeples (*to Dessie*) Jist tell is what the upshot was. I mean
if Joey was willin' to discuss the ins'n'outs of the matter?

Dessie (*like he's pondering*) Er . . .

Steeples Let me huv another go . . . Did it look like he
might be considerin' some sorta compromise solution? Like,
fur instance, you and him getting' together and . . . naw,
forget you an' him getting' together . . . unless you want to
put that on the back burner furra bit? Naw, I can see yur
no' too keen . . . (*Prowling around – brow furrowed.*) so
that's 'compromise' and 'collaboration' ruled out . . .
Lemme think . . . (*Stops pacing.*) Hang on, he didny
actually suggest that you chuck yur hat inty the ring an'
join The Diamonds, by any chance?

Dessie (*wheeling round*) What??

Steeples Because he gave me the impression that . . .

Frankie whispers in his ear.
Dessie takes to drifting around whilst Frankie and
Steeples carry on their whispered conversation – a deal of
nodding and shaking of heads.

(*To Dessie.*) What wur the last words he said to you?

Dessie Last words he said wur 'Over my dead body'.

Steeples Naw, really? (*Turning to Frankie.*) They could be
the last words he ever says to anybody . . . know what I'm
sayin'?

Dessie (*alarmed*) Naw, naw, mebbe I picked him up wrong,
we wur at a funeral, remember . . . Coulda been somethin'
like 'Oh, look . . . over there . . . a dead body' . . . yeh?

Steeples Don't know how come yur tryin' to protect that
palooka, Dessie boy . . . if he was out the road then you an'

the doll could get back together. It was only cos you wur down in the Big Smoke fur all that time that she fell inty his clutches. C'mon, wise up, it's not every day that Eddie Steeples does you a favour, yeh? (*To Frankie.*) Away you in and dial that number . . . know the one I mean?

Dessie (*alarmed*) Naw, wait . . .

Frankie disappears into club.

Steeples Away you an' get a good night's sleep, Des . . . this one's on me.

Lights up on Dessie – we see Donna cross behind.
Donna disappears from sight.
Song: 'It's Only Make Believe' – ensemble.

SCENE TWELVE

Underwood Lane – the early hours of the same night. Dessie at the dimly lit window above the hairdressing salon. The 'OPEN' sign in the club window winks off and on – off and on. A distant clock chimes three times – the 'OPEN' sign winks off and on, off and on – then off. Dessie disappears from window. The club, with Frankie's help, spews out its remaining members, who lurch off this way and that. Dessie appears at the door of the salon and looks out into the deserted street. He draws back into the shadows and lights a cigarette – at that moment two muffled-up guys appear at the far end of the street and make their way towards the club door. Dessie draws deeply on his cigarette and exhales – just as it looks like he's missed spotting the two muffled-up guys he glances into the street – almost chokes. The door to the club opens – the two muffled-up guys are swallowed up. Frankie steps out into the street – Dessie draws back into his hideyhole. Frankie has a swift look both ways along the street and disappears back into the club.

Maureen, in night attire, appears at Dessie's back – puts her chin on Dessie's shoulder. As Dessie jumps so does Maureen.

Maureen *and* **Dessie** Waaaaah!

Maureen God, what a fright you gave us!

Dessie Me?? It was you that gave *us* a fright!

Maureen I was only wonderin' what you wur . . .

Dessie clamps a hand over her mouth.

Dessie I'm waiting fur Joey!

Maureen mumbles something.

To warn him!

Maureen mumbles something.

Cos he's gonny get shot!

Maureen's eyes bulge.

Yeh, that's right . . . *shot* . . . D'you understand how serious this is?? And it's all ma fault . . . Jeesus!

Maureen mumbles something.

Yeh, okay, but see if you make a sound . . .

Removes his hand – Maureen gulps down some air.

Maureen Where is it he's goin' to get shot?

Dessie How should I know?? Possibly kneecap him to stop him makin' a bolt fur it . . . then bring the gun up to his noggin and . . . *BANG!* . . . Bob's yur uncle . . . sorry, yur *dead* uncle.

Maureen He's not getting shot outside Bubble Cuts I hope.

Dessie He's no' gonny get shot outside bloody Bubble Cuts, he's gonny get shot inside Eddie's Nite Club!

Maureen Good, cos ma business would go right down the stank.

Dessie Know what I love about you, Mo?

Maureen Canny be the 'sexual chemicals' I exude, otherwise it would be *you* bangin' at ma bedroom door every night . . . an' not jist ma door either. Naw, what?

Dessie Sorry, I've furgot the question now . . .

Maureen (*sotto voce*) Shhh! Somebody's comin'!

They press themselves into doorway – a shadowy figure appears at the far end of the street.

(*Sotto voce.*) What d'you mean, it was all your fault?

Dessie Shhhhhh!

Maureen (*sotto voce*) An' I want to know what it is you love about me . . . you never answered that one either!

Dessie (*peeking out into the street – sotto voce*) Aw God . . . look who it is!

Maureen Who?

She peeks into the street just as Joey walks into the ghostly pool of light cast by a street lamp.

It's Joey!

Dessie clamps a hand over Maureen's mouth – Joey glances this way and that. Frowns. Walks on.

Dessie (*sotto voce*) I'm supposed to save him, no' you! (*Leaning out of doorway – sotto voce.*) Pssssssssssst!

Joey stops – listens. Club door opens – Frankie looks out.

Frankie Pssssssssssst!

Dessie (*to himself*) That's ma line, ya bastart!

Joey How drunk's a guy's wife got to be to drag him away from a poker game when he's sittin' there wi' a royal flush?? (*Calling through open club door.*) Donna! Get you out here now!

Frankie (*jittery*) C'mon, cool it . . . youse'll wake up the entire neighbourhood . . . (*Puts an arm around Joey's shoulders.*) She's in the dolls' cloakroom.

Steers Joey towards club – Maureen sinks her teeth into Dessie's mitt.

Dessie Ayah, bugger!

Joey (*swinging round*) What was that??

Maureen He's just comin'!

Shoves Dessie into the street.

Dessie Joey! Fancy bumpin' inty you here.

Joey (*shading eyes*) Who is that??

As Joey takes a step towards Dessie, one of the muffled-up guys appears at club doorway – Frankie scoots after Joey.

Frankie C'mon, pal . . . yur wife's waitin' fur you inside. (*Swings him round towards club.*)

At that precise moment, Donna appears at a run at the far end of street – the only person she can see is Dessie in the spill from bedroom above salon.

Donna *Dessie!*

Joey's head jerks round.

Joey Donna??

Dessie Naw, Donna . . . don't! *STOP!!*

A shot rings out. Blackout.
    A Sunday morning nine months and one week later. Eddie's Nite Club is now boarded up, with a scabby sign that reads 'TO LET' which, of course, some 'wag' has

*amended to read 'TOILET'. A carillon of bells from the
church.*

*Dessie appears from number 7 dressed from head to
toe in white (except for his brown shoes) – places a book
in a paper bag.*

*Dessie looks up as the church bells peal, and smiles –
Maureen scurries fast through church gates – points
camera at number 7 Underwood Lane – FLASH!*

(*Smiling.*) Don't be surprised if that doesny come out, Mo.

*A babble of voices as Paula, Gil, Joey, Father Durcan and
Donna spill out of the church passageway into the street
– Donna has a tiny baby wrapped in christening robes in
her arms. Maureen points her camera – FLASH!*

Dessie strolls across to join christening party.

*The godparents, Gil and Paula, position themselves by
Joey's side – Dessie squeezes himself between Father
Durcan and Donna and peers at baby.*

Dessie God help us, he the spittin' image of yur old man.
(*Casting eye at Donna.*)

*Dessie tucks the book in the paper bag into the baby's
shawl. FLASH!*

Maureen Thank you . . . now, could everybody move out
the way so I can get one wi' Donna an' Dessie on thur own?

*Paula, Gil, Father Durcan and Joey move to the side,
leaving Dessie and Donna and the baby while Paula slips
into salon . . . FLASH!*

Great!

*Joey rejoins Donna and baby as Dessie detaches himself
– Paula reappears with a tray of drinks.*

Paula Right . . . who's furra fizzy refreshment??

*Drinks are dispensed – Father Durcan helps himself,
joins Dessie.*

(*Taking her drink from the tray.*) Okay, let's huvva bitta hush fur the godfather!

A ragged cheer as Gil steps forward, glass in hand.

Gil Right . . . before we toast the wean I'd like us to raise wur tumblers to 'absent friends' . . .

All (*raising glasses*) Absent friends!

Dessie (*sniffing the air*) D'you smell somethin' burnin', Father?

Father Durcan ignores the remark and quaffs his bubbly – the door to the closed-down club creaks open and Bruno Fazzi emerges into the street. He surveys the frontage of the former café.

Fazzi (*quietly*) Cazza Madonna . . .

He crosses to stand on the other side of Father Durcan from Dessie. Paula does the rounds topping up glasses – tops Gil up.

Gil Thanks, doll . . . (*Goes to drink.*)

Paula Don't drink that, yuv to toast the baby!

Gil Aw, aye . . . sorry . . . right, Joey, d'you want to . . .?

Joey takes the baby from Donna – the paper bag with the book falls to the ground. Donna retrieves it as Joey holds the baby aloft.

(*Raising glass.*) Ladies an' gentlemen . . . Dessie Diamond.

All (*raising glasses*) Dessie Diamond!

Maureen points her camera – another cheer. FLASH! Dessie joins Donna and puts an arm round her shoulder as she opens The Divine Comedy – *a tear runs down her cheek.*

Dessie See? Told you it wasny all that funny!

Donna looks this way and that – Joey hands baby to Fazzi and joins Donna.

Joey S'up, doll?

Donna (*wiping tears away*) Nothing.

Joey You look like yuv jist seen a ghost.

Donna (*laughing through tears*) I'm fine.

Joey (*tenderly*) Okay . . . lemme get the boy an' we'll go.

He retrieves baby from Fazzi – Donna turns her gaze upwards to the sky.

Donna (*quietly*) Ti amo.

Dessie smilies – Joey gives a puzzled frown, like who did he just take the baby from? Fazzi's face darkens.

Fazzi 'E . . . Donnatella! What I tell you about talkin' wi' scruff??

Dessie (*laughing*) Away to Hell, Fatso! Sorry . . . away *back* to Hell.

Joey (*to Donna*) I'm off to flag down a taxi fur us.

Paula (*to baby*) Bye, doll . . . remember yur Auntie Paula an' yur Uncle Gilbert ur comin' babysit you tonight . . . I'll bring ma drums . . .

Gil (*to baby*) An' I'm bringin' ma big doodah.

Exeunt Joey and baby – Dessie crosses and takes Donna's hand.

Father Durcan (*calling to Joey*) And see that that child's brung up a good Catholic, d'you hear!

Paula Aye, that'll be right. (*Calling to Joey.*) I'll bring ma tape an' measure him up fur that sash we wur talkin' about!

Maureen I wish I hudda baby.

Gil You can huv a shot of ours when we huv one.

Maureen Awright . . . as long as I can do its hair.

Dessie reaches over and kisses Donna's cheek – she puts a hand up and touches the spot.

Song: 'Love Hurts' – ensemble, including Steeples and Frankie in prison garb and handcuffed.

Dessie, in white suit, ascends into Heaven whilst Fazzi, all in black, descends slowly into the fires of Hell . . .

Curtain.

The End.